D0983345

# CHILDREN'S DREAMS

# CHILDREN'S DREAMS

## Understanding the Most Memorable Dreams and Nightmares of Childhood

KELLY BULKELEY
AND
PATRICIA M. BULKLEY

ROWMAN & LITTLEFIELD PUBLISHERS, INC.
*Lanham • Boulder • New York • Toronto • Plymouth, UK*

Published by Rowman & Littlefield Publishers, Inc.
A wholly owned subsidary of
The Rowman & Littlefield Publishing Group, Inc.
4501 Forbes Boulevard, Suite 200, Lanham, Maryland 20706
www.rowman.com

10 Thornbury Road, Plymouth PL6 7PP, United Kingdom

British Library Cataloguing in Publication Information Available

**Library of Congress Cataloging-in-Publication Data**
Bulkeley, Kelly, 1962–
   Children's dreams : understanding the most memorable dreams and
nightmares of childhood / Kelly Bulkeley and Patricia M. Bulkley.
      p.   cm.
   Includes bibliographical references and index.
   ISBN 978-1-4422-1330-2 (cloth : alk. paper) — ISBN 978-1-4422-1332-6
(electronic)
   1. Children's dreams. 2. Dreams—Psychological aspects. I. Bulkley, Patricia
M., 1939– II. Title.
   BF1099.C55B85 2012
   154.6'3083—dc23
                                                          2012020497

∞™ The paper used in this publication meets the minimum requirements of
American National Standard for Information Sciences—Permanence of Paper
for Printed Library Materials, ANSI/NISO Z39.48-1992.

Printed in the United States of America

# CONTENTS

# ACKNOWLEDGMENTS

We are grateful for the love and encouragement of our family—Saylor, Ella, Summer, Amanda, Conor, Alec, Jake, Maya, Dylan, Alex, Kim, Michelle, Kevin, Hilary, and Ned—a large clan always full of good humor and bright ideas. We also appreciate the advice and input of Kalena Babeshoff, John Haule, and Patricia's professional dream group mentors: Nancy, Pat, and Nancy. Sarah Stanton, Jin Yu, and the whole Rowman & Littlefield team have been wonderfully supportive throughout. Finally, we thank the many people who shared their childhood dreams with us—you are the ones who made this book possible!

# INTRODUCTION

Let us begin by imagining what might be going through the mind of a child who wakes up from a dream. Not just any dream, but an especially intense one, the most powerful dream the child has ever experienced. Let's say the child is a girl, five years old, and she awakens early one morning from a very simple dream of a blue snail. A brief, extremely vivid dream image of a blue snail. What do we suppose she's thinking about in those first few moments after she has awakened?

*A blue snail? How strange! There's no such thing.*
*Snails are disgusting! But this one was different . . .*
*Was it real? I can still remember it right now, as clear as anything.*
*Where was I? Did I leave my bedroom and go someplace else?*
*Or did the blue snail come into my bedroom?*
*Will I get to see the blue snail again?*

These are the types of questions that naturally arise when children experience what the depth psychologist C. G. Jung, our primary guide in this book, called "big dreams." At some point virtually every child has an experience like this, an otherworldly dream of wonder and awe that gives rise upon awakening to thoughts, feelings, and reflections that are actually quite profound and even philosophical when you consider them carefully. These questions show that the child's mind is growing in complexity, self-awareness, emotional sensitivity, and intellectual curiosity. In fact, the healthy course of children's psychological development depends on making conceptual leaps exactly like those that occur

1

in big dreams, moving beyond the limits of the here-and-now to think more abstractly, flexibly, symbolically, and creatively. All of these imaginative potentials emerge in the child's mind in response to the wonderfully strange qualities that characterize big dreams.

What happens next? Let's go on to imagine that the girl gets out of bed, goes to find her parents, and tells them about the blue snail. Let's assume she is given some version of the reply that most children in present-day society receive from their parents in a situation like this:

"That's nice, dear. It was just a dream."

*It was just a dream.*

*My parents don't want to talk about it.*

*A dream—that's what you're supposed to call it. A dream.*

*Just a dream.*

*It felt so real! I can still remember it clearly right now. I don't think I'll ever forget it!*

*But it wasn't real. Not like it's real now, when I'm awake.*

*Just a dream. Something you're not supposed to care about.*

*But I care about it. I don't know why, but I do.*

*I'll keep it to myself.*

The child's parents may be thoughtful and loving caregivers with the best of intentions toward their daughter, but they have missed a golden opportunity to nurture and promote the development of her imagination. Without meaning to do so, they have sent a negative message not only about this dream but about dreaming in general. "*It was just a dream.*" The girl learns that her parents, and perhaps all grown-ups, don't pay attention to something that's interesting and meaningful to her. She learns that dreams are not considered a worthwhile topic of thought or conversation. She realizes she is alone in asking those deep questions about where her dream came from. Whatever is happening in her dreams, whatever is creating them, whatever they mean—she is on her own in trying to make sense of it all.

Now let's imagine the parents have some familiarity with children's dreams and their typical patterns. Let's say they know that talking about dreams can be an indirect but deeply honest source of emotional communication between parents and children. Knowing this, they listen with special attention when their daughter describes the dream of the blue snail. They help her feel safe and connected as she wonders about the existential questions raised by her "big dream" experience. They encourage her to stretch her mind to encompass the new perspectives that emerge in her dreams, embracing the creative potential and archetypal wisdom of her own imagination.

This book is dedicated to helping parents follow the alternative path of respecting rather than rejecting the powerful dreams of their children. We offer an approach to interpreting children's night dreams (as distinct from their daydreams and waking fantasies) that is scientifically grounded, easy to apply, and capable of highlighting new powers of creativity emerging in a child's life.

The book is also dedicated to people who received the "it was just a dream" message when they were children and who are still wondering, as adults, about a strange dream from all those years ago. We believe the intense memorability of these kinds of dreams highlights their importance as turning points in a person's psychological and spiritual development, with ongoing relevance for current life.

Finally, we have written this book for teachers, therapists, nurses, counselors, and all other people whose work revolves around the care and education of children. We want to help people in these professions respond effectively when children show an interest in their dreams, learning how to take dreams seriously as expressions of emotional truth rather than dismissing them as sleep-addled nonsense. We offer ideas about how to create safe and stimulating opportunities for children to express their dreams freely, ask honest questions about them, and playfully reflect on their possible meanings.

For all readers, this book is written as a primer on big dreams, those rare but symbolically powerful dreams that make an especially lasting impression on memory and consciousness. Our approach combines the depth psychology of Carl Jung with modern neuroscience and evolutionary theory. Jung (1875–1961) was a Swiss psychiatrist and early follower of Sigmund Freud (1856–1939), the founder of psychoanalysis. Jung went on to develop his own psychological approach, with children's dreams playing a key role in his theory and his clinical practice. Jung developed a method of interpreting early childhood dreams that we have adapted, updated, and refined using new scientific research on brain development and human evolution. The new scientific research puts Jung's ideas on an even stronger foundation and enables us to see how children's dreams emerge not just in connection to the personal life of an individual child but as part of a larger biological drama in which all humans play a role. Each child represents a new chapter in the grand evolutionary tale of our species. Each child's brain develops according to age-old genetic programming that prepares the child for the basic survival challenges of human life. Through their dreams we can learn how children are tapping into those ancient genetic programs, which Jung called the archetypes of the collective unconscious. Our goal is to help you become more fluent with the archetypal language of big dreams in childhood and beyond.

Although we draw inspiration from recent findings in brain-mind research, we believe dream interpretation is more of an art than a science. There is no fixed meaning for any image or symbol in a dream. On the contrary, most dreams have multiple layers of meaning and significance that are densely interwoven with the dreamer's personal life and cultural context. This makes it impossible to say with absolute certainty what any dream does or does not mean. We accept that limitation from the very beginning, and try never to forget it. We do not seek the one "right" interpretation of a dream, and we do not assume we know better than the dreamer what his or her dream might mean. Instead we focus on highlighting special themes, images, and patterns that have recurred across many children's highly memorable dreams. Jung called these recurrent patterns *archetypes* (a term we will explain in more detail in chapter 1), and our approach to dream interpretation explores the potential meanings of these archetypal patterns in relation to the dreamer's current life situation.

Although Jung was a medically trained psychiatrist, he had a deep and sustained interest in religion, mythology, and mystical experience. He recognized that archetypal patterns in dreams arise from the same unconscious realms of the human psyche that also give rise to the symbols found in the world's religious and spiritual traditions. An encounter with archetypal energies can prompt philosophical discoveries and existential insights that transform a person's view of the world. Jung emphasized the fact that very often these psychospiritual energies first emerge in children's dreams. Therefore we should look carefully at the religious and philosophical possibilities of any dream we're trying to interpret, no matter what the background of the dreamer. Not every dream will have these profound dimensions of meaning, but when it's a "big" dream it's worth paying attention to these deeper potentials.

Our academic training is in religious studies, Kelly as a psychologist of religion and Patricia as a Presbyterian minister. We agree with Jung that children's big dreams often touch on issues of religion, spirituality, and philosophy, and we agree that such dreams can appear in any family setting, whether the child is being raised as an atheist, a member of a faith tradition, or anything else. We are not advocating a specific religious point of view about what dreams mean or where they come from. Instead, we are using our religious studies background to help illuminate aspects of children's dreams that might not be obvious to people unfamiliar with spiritual traditions around the world and through history.

We consider ourselves *pragmatists* in that we set aside questions of where dreams come from and emphasize instead the impact of dreams on people's emotions, thoughts, and behaviors. Pragmatism, as conceived by philosopher William James, examines human experiences in terms of their "fruits": what they lead to, what they produce or generate, how they influence life for better or worse. Big dreams are especially "fruitful" in terms of their long-term influence on consciousness. The more we know about these kinds of dreams, the more we and our children can benefit from them. In the pages to come we will describe three pragmatic fruits that frequently emerge from children's big dreams.

First is a lifelong feeling of *wonder*. These strange, surprising, awe-inspiring dreams expand children's sense of possibility, opening their minds to alternative realities and different ways of looking at the world. Big dreams fundamentally transform children's awareness of themselves and the world around them.

Second is a new recognition of interpersonal *connections*, the deep bonds of relationship that make family and social life possible. Big dreams can reveal areas of previously unknown connections or signal the need to develop new connections as part of healthy growth. Parents who want to build and sustain good long-term relations with their children will find big dreams to be a valuable ally in that process.

Third is a *preparation* for future challenges. Big dreams can anticipate difficult situations children often face in their waking lives and guide them toward creative responses. In this sense big dreams can work like an early warning system, alerting children (and their parents) to possible problems ahead and providing instinctual guidance for dealing with those problems if and when they actually arise.

The dream interpretations we offer in this book revolve around these three themes—wonder, connections, preparation—and their pragmatic impact on the dreamer. We show that dream interpretation is not merely idle navel-gazing. It is a natural and scientifically legitimate means of unleashing our brain's innate power of creative imagination.

If you are a person who prefers to learn by doing, you may want to skip straight to chapter 3, where we begin exploring and interpreting the big dream reports we have gathered from a variety of sources. If you are a person who learns best from a step-by-step approach, you will find in chapters 1 and 2 an outline of the basic principles we use to interpret the dreams in later chapters.

Chapter 1 introduces the archetypal theory of Jung and his basic method for interpreting children's dreams. We will explain key Jungian ideas such as archetypes, the collective unconscious, the ego, amplification, projection, "big" and "little" dreams, compensation, and the anticipatory function. We do not consider Jung an all-knowing source of absolute truth, but we do believe his work on children's dreams offers an excellent point of departure for the pragmatic approach we are offering.

If we had written this book ten or fifteen years ago, we would not have needed a second chapter on dreaming and the brain in early life. But in recent years many important discoveries about human mental life have come from neuroscience and cognitive psychology. We now know more than ever before about the healthy growth of children's brains and the factors that help or hinder their growth. If our goal is to understand the nature and meaning of children's dreams, we have to account for the latest scientific research on how the brain develops from the beginning of life through adolescence. More than that, we have to look at child development in light of current theories of evolution so we can understand why our species has evolved with an *imagination*, the extremely valuable ability (apparently unique to humans) to create complex mental simulations of possible realities. When we look at children's dreams in this bigger scientific context, we can appreciate them better as natural expressions of a highly evolved, species-wide, hard-wired feature of healthy brain-mind functioning.

The principles of interpretation outlined in chapters 1 and 2 are applied in the next three chapters to several dozen children's dreams we have gathered through personal contacts and various sources of research. These chapters are organized by age groups, to make it easier to highlight the connections between dream content and the developmental challenges of particular eras of childhood. Chapter 3 looks at dreams from very early in childhood, in the three- to five-year-old range, when self-awareness first begins to dawn. Chapter 4 presents the dreams of children from the ages of five to nine, when they have entered formal schooling and begun adapting to a bigger social world. Chapter 5 looks at the dreams of older children and adolescents, as puberty approaches and their minds, bodies, and social interactions begin to undergo dramatic changes.

In each of these chapters we show how to apply a basic method of interpretation that makes it relatively easy to identify the archetypal themes in the dreams and understand their relevance to waking life. We do not offer complete and exhaustive interpretations of these dreams, which would be foolish to attempt, impossible to achieve, and boring to read. We offer a more focused kind of analysis, concentrating on aspects of meaning that relate to basic instinctual concerns shared by virtually all humans.

Chapter 6 provides a summary of our ideas about cultivating a healthy imagination in childhood and beyond, with special attention to issues faced by teachers and therapists. We explain how to respond with empathy and insight when another person, whether a child or adult, shares a dream with you. We discuss the vital importance of sleep in child development and what adults can do to help children sleep more soundly. Children who do not sleep well are not likely to dream well, either, and children who do not dream well are cut off from their own inner powers of creativity and emotional intelligence. Parents can give their children a lifelong gift by helping them establish good sleep patterns and dreaming self-awareness early in life.

In the appendixes we provide a list of the dreams presented through the book along with some suggestions about good children's stories involving dream adventures. We have included a lengthy analysis of the dreams and nightmares of Harry Potter in J. K. Rowling's fantasy book series, which we hope will give parents and teachers a good resource for initiating conversations with their children about Harry's dreams and what they might mean. Another appendix provides a list of simple activities to stimulate wonder in childhood. The final appendix provides sample questions that can be used for a study group or book club discussion about this book.

Jung said that highly memorable dreams from childhood represent "the richest jewels in the treasure house of the soul." This evocative phrase beautifully conveys the spirit in which we have written *Children's Dreams*. These vibrant creations of a child's budding imagination should not be dismissed as random nonsense, but rather welcomed and celebrated as expressions of the powerful potential within each human mind.

# 1

# INTERPRETING
# CHILDREN'S DREAMS:
# AN ARCHETYPAL APPROACH

Carl Jung grew up in rural Switzerland in the late nineteenth century. None of the technologies of modern life had yet been invented, and he enjoyed a childhood immersed in the natural glories of the lakes, mountains, forests, and valleys of the Swiss Alps. When he finally sat down to tell his life story (published in 1961 as *Memories, Dreams, Reflections*), Jung started by describing the earliest dream he could remember, a mysterious revelation that became a lifelong touchstone for his psychological and spiritual approach to the world. He says the dream came when he was between three and four years old, and it starts in a familiar field near his home:

> Suddenly I discovered a dark, rectangular, stone-lined hole in the ground. I had never seen it before. I ran forward curiously and peered down into it. Then I saw a stone stairway leading down. Hesitantly and fearfully, I descended. At the bottom was a doorway with a round arch, closed off by a green curtain. It was a big, heavy curtain of worked stuff like brocade, and it looked very sumptuous. Curious to see what might be hidden behind, I pushed it aside. I saw before me in the dim light a rectangular chamber about thirty feet long. The ceiling was arched and of hewn stone. The floor was laid with flagstones, and in the center a red carpet ran from the entrance to a low platform. . . . Something was standing on it which I thought at first was a tree trunk twelve to fifteen feet high and about one and a half to two feet thick. It was a huge thing,

reaching almost to the ceiling. But it was of a curious compo-
sition: it was made of skin and naked flesh, and on top there
was something like a rounded head with no face and no hair.
. . . On the very top of the head was a single eye, gazing mo-
tionlessly upward. . . . I was paralyzed with terror. At that moment I heard from outside and above me my mother's voice.
She called out, "Yes, just look at him. That is the man-eater!"

This haunting dream remained a clear memory in Jung's
mind until the end of his life more than eighty years later. Looking back on it, he marveled at how the images had no source
in his daily experiences as a young child—the dream seemed to
come from someplace else entirely. He described it as a sudden,
unexpected, but ultimately beneficial transformation of his young
consciousness:

> Who spoke to me then? Who talked of problems far beyond
> my knowledge? Who brought the Above and Below together,
> and laid the foundation for everything that was to fill the sec-
> ond half of my life with stormiest passion? Who but that alien
> guest who came both from above and from below? Through
> this childhood dream I was initiated into the secrets of the
> earth. What happened then was a kind of burial in the earth,
> and many years were to pass before I came out again. Today
> I know that it happened in order to bring about the greatest
> possible amount of light into the darkness. It was an initiation
> into the realm of darkness. My intellectual life had its uncon-
> scious beginnings at that time.

An entire book could be devoted to the full text of this
one remarkable dream and its far-ranging impact on Jung's life
and later psychological theories. For our purposes, we just want
to point out the dream's relevance for understanding why Jung
claimed that early childhood dreams were so important. He knew
from direct personal experience that unusually memorable and
symbolically complex dreams can be vital turning points in a

child's psychological development, with meaningful consequences unfolding throughout a lifetime.

When Jung grew up he studied medicine in college and then trained as a clinical psychiatrist working to heal people of their mental illnesses. He formed a close relationship with Sigmund Freud, the founder of psychoanalysis and author of *The Interpretation of Dreams* in 1900. Together Freud and Jung developed a new model of the human mind that emphasized the influence of unconscious instincts, memories, and feelings on conscious mental life. After splitting with Freud in 1914, in part over their differing approaches to dreams, Jung pursued his own ideas about how the mind works. He coined several terms that have become a common part of our language today: archetype, synchronicity, collective unconscious, projection, extravert, introvert. Jung's psychological theory provides the basis for the widely used Myers-Briggs personality test as well as the twelve-step program of Alcoholics Anonymous.

Jung does not have all the answers to all questions about dreams. In addition to his work we draw on the ideas of many other dream researchers, including Freud, Harry Hunt, Antti Revonsuo, G. William Domhoff, Ernest Hartmann, Kate Adams, Jeremy Taylor, Montague Ullman, Clara Hill, and the community of researchers in the International Association for the Study of Dreams. Nevertheless, we do feel that Jung's ideas are especially helpful in the process of exploring children's dreams. We appreciate his openness to the idea that dreams have spiritual value for the dreamers, although as a psychologist he admitted he could not say anything definite about the reality or truth of particular spiritual beliefs. Both of those points will be emphasized throughout our book: the spiritual potential of children's dreams *and* the limits of what we can say about that potential. The big dreams of childhood, whatever their cause and wherever they come from, have a powerful impact on how people look at life, often in ways relating to the great existential questions of religion and philosophy. Jung understood this dimension of dreaming because of his personal experience as well as his psychiatric work in a mental health clinic. We believe his ideas are as helpful today as they were in his lifetime, especially in light of recent developments in cognitive science and evolutionary theory.

## JUNG'S SEMINARS ON CHILDHOOD DREAMS

Jung taught the basic principles of interpreting children's dreams in a series of graduate school seminars in Zurich in 1936–1940. A new translation of the lectures and class discussions appeared in 2008, opening the way to a better understanding of the actual practice of Jungian dream interpretation. The seminars offer a fascinating portrait of Jung as a down-to-earth human being (he swears, cracks jokes, tells politically incorrect stories, and sharply scolds one of his students). The seminars are also very long, dense, and filled with technical terms, making the book a tough slog for people who do not have prior familiarity with Jung's ideas.

We have taken the past two years to study the seminars very closely, thinking about how to adapt Jung's approach to help people today who educate and care for children. Jung's students in the seminar were mostly clinicians and medical professionals, but the essential simplicity of his method allows anyone to use it and benefit from it. You do not need to be a licensed doctor or therapist to interpret children's dreams. Children do not need to be suffering from mental health problems before it's worth paying attention to their dreaming experiences. Our book aims to expand the application of Jung's methods to all children, showing that big dreams are natural, healthy expressions of psychological growth and spiritual discovery.

## THE COLLECTIVE UNCONSCIOUS AND CULTURE

To make it easier to gain a big picture view of Jung's theory, we have created a series of graphics representing the trajectory of hu-

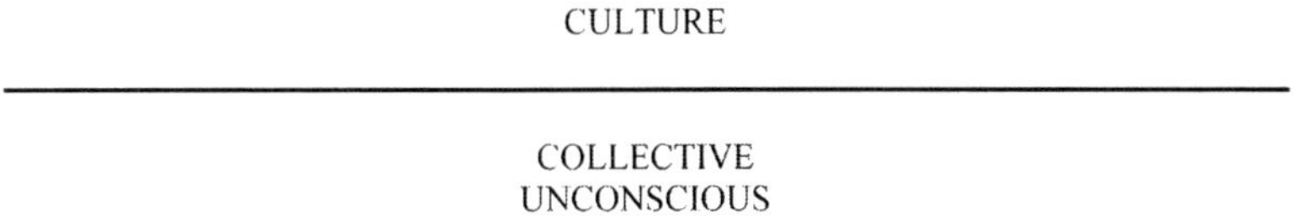

CULTURE

COLLECTIVE
UNCONSCIOUS

**Figure 1. Prior to Birth**

man development across the life span. Figure 1 shows the preexisting background to any individual's life, the basic context into which every human is born. Prior to the birth of any individual person, there exist two spheres of distinctively human reality: the collective unconscious and culture.

The starting premise of Jung's psychology is that the human mind is not a blank slate, devoid of content or purpose. On the contrary, the mind of a newborn human is highly structured, powerfully functioning, and predisposed to seek out other people. From the moment of birth we are yearning for interaction with the world. Our minds are primed to respond adaptively to the kinds of situations and challenges humans typically face in life. The *collective unconscious* is Jung's term for this shared psychological foundation of our species. The collective unconscious represents the deepest level of the human mind, a level that's connected to our bodies, our biological drives, and the evolved nature of the brain (more of which we will discuss in the next chapter).

Jung told his students in the seminars: "The collective unconscious is simply the psychic expression of the identity of brain structure irrespective of all racial differences." Just as the basic building plan of the human body includes two arms, two legs, a spine, and so on, the basic building plan of the human mind includes a variety of instinctual tendencies to perceive, feel, think, and behave in certain ways in certain situations. Jung said these instinctual tendencies are rooted in biological processes reaching far back into the prehistory of our species: "[T]he unconscious is older than consciousness. . . . The unconscious is what is originally given, from which consciousness rises anew again and again."

## ARCHETYPES

When speaking of these innate psychological tendencies in the collective unconscious, Jung used the term *archetypes*. In this book we use the term "archetypal" to speak of basic instinctual patterns, genetically inscribed in the brain, that enable us to satisfy the biological needs and developmental yearnings of our species. Archetypal energies come from the "ground up": they are rooted in nature, in our bodies, and in the neurological networks of our brains. They are preparatory patterns of thought that orient our minds to focus on aspects of life that are especially important for our well-being.

For example, the four classic elements of water, fire, earth, and air often elicit archetypal feelings in people. (We will describe several dreams of water and fire later in the book.) These elements have been a part of human life as far back in evolutionary history as we care to look, and thus our brains have become adaptively prepared to perceive, observe, and interact with them. When each of us enters the world we already "know" something about water, fire, air, and earth. Our unconscious minds already understand the importance of these elements in life, priming us to benefit from their values and guard against their dangers.

Another example of archetypal patterns we will discuss throughout this book revolves around family relations. The exact shape of what counts as a family varies from culture to culture, but throughout history humans have typically grown up in small kin groups of parents, siblings, and other relatives. Humans are an innately social species from birth onward, a fact that has stamped itself deeply in the evolution of the brain. Again, we are born already "knowing" how to interact in a family environment; we are primed to perceive, communicate, think, remember, and behave adaptively within a family context, whatever form it takes.

When archetypal material emerges in the mind it usually brings a strong emotional charge that can be startling and decentering. Not unreasonably, people often feel surprised and alarmed when something bursts into conscious awareness from an unknown source. They may be disturbed by the realization that their egos are not entirely in charge of what happens in their minds. Although the unconscious energy of the archetypes may initially seem frightening, we agree with Jung that their ultimate value is to guide each individual's psychological development according to the ancient evolutionary wisdom of our species.

## CULTURE

*Culture* is the whole range of community beliefs and practices that influence what shape a particular human's life will take. This includes the details of where you were born, in which period of history, in what kind of family, telling what kinds of stories, keeping what kinds of secrets, playing what kinds of games, using what languages in what situations, practicing what kinds of rituals, following or reacting against what religious beliefs, and so forth. All of these influences and more make up the cultural matrix into which every human is born.

The collective unconscious includes all potentialities of human psychology. Culture is where those potentialities are actualized.

## THE EGO

Figure 2 adds to figure 1 by showing the life span of an individual who is born into these two realities. The arc moving from left to right represents the growth of the *ego*, the "me" of conscious life. The ego is the center of waking personality. In the early years of life it's important to build up a stable and strong ego to meet the challenges of life. Preschool children need a healthy ego to control

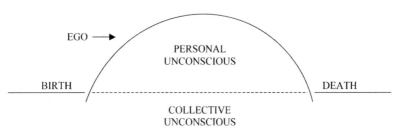

EGO ⟶

PERSONAL
UNCONSCIOUS

BIRTH                                                        DEATH

COLLECTIVE
UNCONSCIOUS

**Figure 2.  Ego Development**

their impulses and play well with others. Elementary school children need a healthy ego to focus their attention on learning the basic skills of society (such as reading, mathematics, and science). Teenagers need a healthy ego to make good decisions in morally ambiguous situations. Our minds are predisposed to create a central core of personal identity that organizes our perceptions, thinks about our goals, plans our actions, and regulates our behavior.

As children grow up their egos learn how to adjust the ancient desires of our species to the particular realities of *this* culture, *this* place, *this* time, *this* set of circumstances. Although too much ego control over the unconscious can lead to problems (some cases of which we will discuss later in the book), a well-developed ego gives people more coherence in their psychological functioning and more effectiveness in achieving their goals.

In Buddhism, Hinduism, and several other religious traditions the goal is to diminish or dissolve the dominance of the individual ego, so it might sound odd to talk about the importance of building it up. There is a difference, however, between the developmental needs of children and the spiritual practices of mature adults. What is healthy and appropriate for one may not be so for the other. The kind of ego development we are discussing does not impede later spiritual pursuits. Instead it creates a foundation of adaptive functioning that prepares a person for the emergent qualities of mature spirituality.

Later in life, perhaps after retirement, many people experience (and enjoy) a decreasing interest in ego-driven activities and a rising interest in activities that transcend individual concerns and relate to the traditions of their family, community, and human-kind as a whole. The downward direction in the second half of the arc in figure 2 is not meant to signal a predetermined decline of energy or meaning in this phase of life. The arc represents the lessening of a need to build up the ego by the time one reaches midlife. At that point, many people shift their psychological energies toward broader concerns beyond the limits of their individual egos.

The trajectory of a person's life is never simple or easily represented. Figure 2 is obviously not drawn to scale, but we hope it illustrates the rapid rise of ego consciousness in child development. Many of the dreams we look at later in the book will revolve around the obstacles, dangers, and anxieties children face in forming a healthy ego.

As the individual's ego develops in childhood and beyond, the memories and experiences of that person's life combine, or "constellate" as Jung would say, to form a part of the psyche called the *personal unconscious*. The personal unconscious reflects the autobiographical details that are specific to your life. They are *your* memories, not collective memories, although the boundary between the personal and collective unconscious is always porous and permeable to some degree. This is why the horizontal line in figure 2 has become dotted, to show the interaction between the two dimensions of the unconscious. In healthy psychological functioning the archetypal instincts continually flow into our minds, and our minds continually learn how better to channel, direct, and benefit from those instincts.

## DREAMING

This is where dreams come into play, as shown in figure 3. When we are awake, ego consciousness maintains control of the mind. It focuses on external reality, constantly surveying our physical surroundings, analyzing our social situations, and planning our next

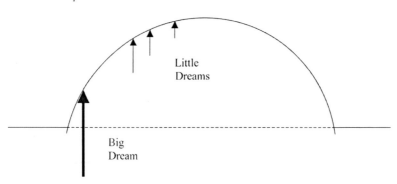

**Figure 3.   Dreams**

actions. But when we go to sleep, all of that changes. We withdraw our senses from the world, surrender the ego's strict supervision of our thoughts, and reenter a psychological realm that is rooted in the evolutionary history of our species. Dreams are a nightly revival of the unconscious mind. In dreams the ego recedes and the energies of the unconscious come to the fore. Dreaming takes place in a kind of middle zone between waking consciousness and the unfathomable depths of the collective psyche.

Jung took special interest in *big dreams* because they directly connect the individual to the tremendous power and wisdom of the collective unconscious. He contrasted them with *little dreams*, which are more common, less memorable, and not as existentially significant. Little dreams stem from the personal unconscious, with content relating to current activities and daily concerns. They may be meaningful but do not make the same impact on people's minds as big dreams. We certainly do not want to diminish anyone's attention to little dreams, which have many gifts to bear. But we agree with Jung that rare, extremely vivid, highly memorable dreams deserve special attention as expressions of the deepest powers of the unconscious mind. This is why people often say their big dreams feel as if they came from some place outside themselves, from a place very different from their regular dreams. From Jung's perspective that is actually a true statement in the sense that big dreams do indeed emerge from a part of the mind very different from the waking ego or the personal unconscious.

Some people remember dreams nearly every night, while others remember only one or two a year, if that. In Jung's approach the *quantity* of dream recall does not matter. What matters is the *quality* of your understanding of the few dreams you do remember. Just one big dream can become a lifelong treasure of creative insight.

## NIGHTMARES

Big dreams often take the form of nightmares, with intensely negative emotions (fear, anger, sadness), aggressive interactions, and harmful misfortunes. One of the most paradoxical ideas in Jung's theory is that nightmares can be valuable sources of psychological growth. The natural temptation is to shy away from nightmares, as we shy away from anything that seems dangerous or threatening. Indeed, the most likely situation for parents to use the "it was just a dream" line is when their children have woken up in the middle of the night from a bad dream. Most parents will say or do anything to comfort a sobbing, terrified child, and it certainly can be helpful for children who have just had a nightmare to recognize the difference between what was happening in the dream and what's happening now, in the arms of their parents. However, from Jung's point of view we can see nightmares as dreams in which especially strong archetypal materials have emerged that frighten the ego precisely because they are so strange, powerful, and alien. The dreams are scary because they overwhelm the ego—but if the ego can learn to expand its range of awareness to include these new archetypal energies, the result can be a lessening of fear and a new burst of psychological growth. In later chapters we will show several examples of nightmares with these growth-promoting qualities.

Jung taught that nightmares often arise as a symptom of incomplete integration, an unhealthy split of consciousness and the collective unconscious. This is why his therapeutic approach to nightmares was to encourage the dreamer to accept the frightening elements as parts of themselves. Jung said to his students, "A persecutory dream always means: *This* wants to come to me. . . . You would like to split it off, you experience it as something alien—but it just becomes all the more dangerous."

Jung's interpretations of early childhood nightmares concentrate on identifying which aspects of the unconscious are symbolized in the nightmares and helping the dreamer find a way to heal the split between consciousness and those alienated parts of the psyche. Instead of fighting against such inner psychological powers, Jung advocated accepting and embracing them: "The best stance would be: 'Please, come and devour me!'"

That's easier said than done, of course, but we believe Jung's interpretive principle is important to remember: Nightmares can reveal aspects of the mind that need to be better integrated into the dreamer's conscious personality.

The healthy development of a child's mind depends on balancing the demands of both consciousness and the collective unconscious, making sure the ego grows up to be stable, secure, competent, adaptive, and resilient, while maintaining a free flow of emotional energy and instinctual wisdom from the unconscious. A failure to balance the demands of conscious and unconscious life lies at the root of many people's psychological problems, Jung said, and he looked to children's dreams as early warning signs of conflicts and tendencies that may, if left unaddressed, lead to problems later in life.

As we noted in the introduction, Jung also emphasized the preparatory value of dreams in terms of spiritual growth and insight. The big dreams of childhood can give people their first glimpses of transcendence, their first encounters with sacred powers and mind-stretching possibilities, their first feelings of profound wonder. The spiritual path of a person's life often begins with such experiences.

## INTERPRETING DREAMS

Let's get very practical now. When Jung set out to interpret a particular dream, he said, "I proceed from the very simple principle that I understand nothing of the dream, do not know what it means, and do not conceive an idea of how the dream image is embedded in each person's mind." This might sound like a surprising admission from one of history's all-time great dream experts, but Jung insisted that we have to start the process of dream interpretation with a humbling admission of ignorance. Every dream is a unique creation of an individual's imagination. We do not know at the outset how the dream relates to that person's life, so we have to keep an open mind and approach the dream with curiosity, respect, and a willingness to accept ambiguity and paradox. Most important, we must listen very closely to the dream itself. Jung told his students, "In this I rely on a Jewish authority, the Talmud, where it says: 'The dream is its own interpretation,' meaning that we have to take the dream for what it is."

Dreams appear strange and hard to understand not because there are random nonsense from a sleep-impaired brain (one of the biggest misconceptions about dreaming) but because our rational minds struggle to decipher the symbolic language of the unconscious. Jung said in another of his works, "To me dreams are a part of nature, which harbors no intention to deceive, but expresses something as best it can, just as a plant grows or an animal seeks food as best it can." If we want to discover what dreams mean, we must learn to understand their natural language, the language of images, symbols, feelings, and metaphors.

The best way to do this, Jung said, is by using the technique of amplification—"I amplify an existing image until it becomes visible." This technique involves circling around the dream from multiple angles, considering each element by itself and in relation to the dream as a whole. To amplify the dream is to highlight its possible connections with archetypal themes in myths, fables, folklore, literature, and art. These connections help the dreamer find the meanings that are most relevant to his or her personal life situation.

Jung spoke of two general functions of dreams that he saw at work in people's dreams. One we have already mentioned, the *prospective* function: Dreams have a powerful capacity to prepare people for likely challenges in their waking lives. The other function is *compensation*: Dreams tend to bring forth unconscious material that has been ignored or repressed by the conscious mind. These two functions, the prospective and compensatory, will be illustrated in several of the dreams discussed in chapters 3–5.

The interpretation of a dream usually leads to more questions than answers. It is not a mathematical equation with a single objective solution. Jung made sure to caution his students about expecting too much or getting carried away:

> We will see how far we will get with it. We will not always come to a satisfactory solution. The purpose of this seminar is to practice on the basis of the material. The point is not to worm out brilliant interpretations through speculations. We have to content ourselves with recognizing the symbols in their wider psychological context, and thus find our way into the psychology of the dreamer.

When interpreting a dream, how much input is needed from the dreamer? With little dreams, the contents relate primarily to personal memories and experiences from that individual's life. It can be difficult to interpret those kinds of dreams without extensive input from the dreamer. With big dreams, the situation is different. There may be some personal content, but most if not all of the content comes from outside the sphere of personal experience. The dreamer has few if any associations, and can't easily explain where the dream came from. This is a sign the dream has an archetypal dimension that can be amplified and interpreted without as much personal input. Some big dreams have elements of personal content, and a complete interpretation would include that information. But the level of interpretation we are discussing in this book focuses on the archetypal aspects and for the most part leaves aside the personal context. That's the method Jung was teaching in his seminar: How to discern archetypal symbolism in the big dreams of childhood. He left it to the clinical practices of his students, as we leave it to our readers, to apply this method in a way that's sensitive to each unique child's life context.

## THE FOUR-PART TEMPLATE

One of the tools Jung gave his students was a four-part template for analyzing a dream report at the outset of the interpretation process. He saw dreams as symbolically equivalent to plays and dramatic performances, and so he took ideas from the world of theater to divide each dream into four elements:

1. *Locale*: The place and time of the dream and a list of the characters.
2. *Exposition*: The situation at the start of the dream, the beginning of the plot.
3. *Peripeteia*: How the plot develops, where it goes, what changes.
4. *Lysis*: The result, solution, closure; how it ends.

Jung said, "Most dreams show this dramatic structure," although he emphasized that some dreams do not have a clear-cut lysis or conclusion, which can be a sign of an unresolved conflict. In the dream examples we discuss in chapters 3–5 we use this four-part dramatic schema exactly as Jung did, as a map to orient ourselves when first encountering a dream and initially assessing its content.

The next chapter brings Jung's approach up to date with modern neuroscience and evolutionary science. It shows why children's dreams are an underappreciated feature of early life development and how the latest evidence of brain-mind research supports an appreciation for the instinctual wisdom of big dreams in childhood. If you are comfortable with the theory and would rather get right to the dreams and the practice of interpretation, you can skip chapter 2 for now and read it later. This chapter has given you the key ideas of our method, which we show you how to apply starting in chapter 3.

# 2

# BRAIN SCIENCE, DREAMS, AND THE IMAGINATION

After spending so much time on Jung, it's fair to ask why we should listen to the psychological theories of someone who died more than fifty years ago, before the revolutionary discoveries of modern neuroscience. Scientific knowledge of the brain has advanced so much in the half century since Jung's death that we have to question whether his ideas are still relevant. Why should we keep paying attention to someone most neuroscientists seem to have left behind?

The short answer is, we should pay attention to any psychological theory, no matter how old, if it leads to beneficial effects in our lives. A newer theory is not necessarily a more fruitful theory.

The longer answer, which we lay out in this chapter, is that recent findings in brain science actually support Jung's approach to children's dreams. His ideas are surprisingly compatible with scientific research, including the latest findings about the genetic foundations of human development, the biological processes shaping evolutionary history, the role of sleep in neurological growth, and the typical patterns of dreaming in childhood. This information strengthens the central idea in our book: Dreaming contributes to the healthy growth of children's imaginations. The latest evidence shows that dreaming is a naturally creative expression of the brain's activities during sleep.

We discuss six areas where scientific research relates most directly to children's dreams: brain structure, social cognition, sleep, play, emotion, and metaphor. In each of these areas we discuss findings that help us better understand the dynamics of children's dreaming. We will not dive too deeply into the technical details, although readers curious to learn more can find good sources in the references at the end of the book. The goal here is to provide enough scientific information to justify a serious interest in children's dreams, whether you are guided by Jungian psychology or some other theory.

## THE BRAIN

First, let's look at current findings about the structure of the human brain. Our species does not have the biggest brain—dolphins and whales have larger brains than ours with more overall volume. But humans do have the greatest brain size relative to body size. Compared to other primate species, our brains have an unusually large development of the cerebral cortex, also known as the neocortex. This is the newest part of the brain in evolutionary terms, and unlike the rest of the brain it is not specifically dedicated to preset instinctual tasks or behaviors. It represents a kind of "free" brain power, a source of extra neurological space available for new learning, expanded memory storage, and much more complex forms of mental analysis and evaluation.

The neocortex has dramatically enhanced the human brain's potential for neural connectivity. It gives us a mental processing power that no other creature seems to have. Our brains contain approximately one trillion neurons, most of which are connected to thousands and thousands of other neurons, all talking back and forth to each other in a fluid, ever-changing, multilayered language of chemical and electrical signals. Neurons connect to each other in local clusters and in networks stretching across the brain. Each neuron participates in many different systems, changing its behavior in response to what other neurons are doing from one moment to the next. The overall complexity of these interactions is simply astounding. Neuroscientists themselves admit to feelings of awe as they contemplate the vast number of possible neural connections the human brain can generate. According to Richard H. Thompson in his book *The Brain: A Neuroscience Primer,* "The number of *possible* different combinations of connections among the neurons in a single human brain is larger than the total number of atomic particles that make up the known universe. Hence the diversity of the interconnections in a human brain seems almost without limit."

This basic finding of modern brain science underscores our claim about the power of the human imagination. The immense processing capacity of the human neocortex provides the neural basis for imagining future possibilities, envisioning alternative scenarios, and formulating long-range goals. We have the ability to imagine, and to dream, because we have brains that facilitate free, wide-ranging associations across many different neural systems.

The neocortex has grown around an older core of brain structure that we share with other mammals, reptiles, birds, and even fish. In a very real sense, the ancient instinctual drives of these creatures live within us. We are born with their evolutionary history woven into the fabric of our physical and psychological being. This is why modern brain scientists have insisted that the human mind is not a blank slate, not a tabula rasa empty of all content. The evidence from evolution shows that our brains are genetically programmed with a set of innate predispositions that guide our development and shape our behavior in life. These predispositions revolve around the basic survival concerns shared by virtually all creatures: growing to maturity, defending against predators, finding a mate, protecting our young. The neocortex allows us flexibility in how we express these instinctual desires, but even our "highest" thoughts and loftiest ideals are grounded in the age-old realities of our animal nature.

These instinctual tendencies are not usually part of ordinary conscious awareness. They operate unconsciously, in networks of the brain that follow the guidance not of the waking ego but of the biological imperatives underlying all life. A major theme of modern neuroscience is the importance of unconscious brain activity and its roots in evolution. To use an image that goes back at least to Freud, the conscious ego is but the tip of the mental iceberg, with the vast majority of brain functioning taking place below the surface in the unconscious. Neuroscientist John Bargh, in a book he coedited called *The New Unconscious*, said, "People are often unaware of the reasons and causes of their own behavior. In fact, recent experimental evidence points to a deep and fundamental dissociation between conscious awareness and the mental processes responsible for one's behavior; many of the wellsprings of behavior appear to be opaque to conscious access." In his book *The Feeling of What Happens*, neuroscientist Antonio Damasio makes a similar point, connecting Freud's early ideas about the unconscious with current brain-mind research:

> The world of the psychoanalytic unconscious has its roots in the neural systems which support autobiographical memory. . . . The unconscious, in the narrow meaning in which the word has been etched in our culture, is only a part of the vast amount of processes and contents that remain nonconscious, not known in core or extended consciousness. In fact, the list of the "not known" is astounding. Consider what it includes:
>
> 1. all the fully formed images to which we do not attend;
> 2. all the neural patterns that never become images;
> 3. all the dispositions that were acquired through experience, lie dormant, and may never become an explicit neural pattern;
> 4. all the quiet remodeling of such dispositions and all their quiet renetworking—that may never become explicitly known; and
> 5. all the hidden wisdom and know-how that nature embodied in innate, homeostatic dispositions.

Amazing, indeed, how little we ever know.

All of this new scientific information harmonizes remarkably well with Jung's ideas about the collective unconscious and the archetypes. Neuroscientists are showing in more detail than ever before the deep roots of human mental life in the ancient instinctual drives that are born within each child's brain. This is exactly what Jung meant by the collective unconscious! Therefore we will now use that term to refer not just to Jung's theory but to the general findings of current neuroscience. Likewise, we will follow not only Jung but also the mainstream of modern brain science to say that an image or experience is "archetypal" when it connects us with the powerful unconscious drives that stem from the evolutionary history of our species.

## SOCIAL COGNITION

As researchers have looked in more detail at the innate structures of the human brain, they have found that enormous resources are devoted to preparing us for life in a complex social environment. We enter life ready to use language, form relationships with other people, and analyze the nuances and subtleties of community interactions. Long ago the ancient Greek philosopher Aristotle stated, "Man is a social animal," and modern brain scientists are proving the truth of his insight. Indeed, a growing subfield is known as "social neuroscience," in recognition of the fact that the human brain never develops in isolation but always within a relational context—within a family, neighborhood, tribe, village, city, state, or some other form of social grouping. When babies are deprived of regular social interaction and interpersonal contact, their mental growth suffers terribly. Newborn humans innately seek out a living emotional connection with their caregivers because that kind of social contact is necessary to activate their innate mental powers. Evolution has programmed our brains to be ready for, and to thrive within, a world of rich social activity.

One of the great ironies of modern neuroscience is that by focusing on the individual brain we have discovered a new appreciation for society, community, and the relational nature of healthy human life. The British psychoanalyst D. W. Winnicott once said there is no such thing as just a baby, but always a baby-and-mother. In a similar vein we believe there is no such thing as just a brain, but always a brain-in-society. The latest research findings indicate that it simply makes no sense to speak of human brain functions apart from the formative influence of social interactions in our early development.

This idea fits very well with Jung's notion of culture as the arena in which the individual emerges into conscious life. We are born with general guidance from the collective unconscious, but we have to fill in the archetypal potentials with our experiences and relationships with other people. The human mind grows in response to others, in relationship with the social world. When we interact with people and form emotional bonds with them, we literally change the neural wiring of the brain and activate instinctual programs that have been designed by evolution to enhance our successful adaptation to life.

The genetic architecture of our brains assumes that we will be raised in social groups. Human beings are an innately relational species, dependent on close interactions with other people from birth onward. We may not be the fastest or strongest animals, but our culturally enhanced brains have proven to be very powerful tools for accomplishing our evolutionary goals of survival and reproduction.

## SLEEP

All mammals have the same basic sleep patterns as we do, and birds and reptiles have periods of rest that can be considered "proto-sleep." Evolution has clearly established the waking-sleeping cycle as a fundamental pattern of healthy human life. No one can survive without *any* sleep. People can delay or minimize the amount of time they sleep, but if they push it too far they suffer as a result. Numerous studies have shown that sleep-deprived people have problems with thinking and problem-solving, emotional self-control, physical coordination, and immunological health. The electronic distractions of the modern world have made it harder than ever to get a decent night's rest, but scientific research leaves no doubt that our brains function at their best when we regularly get an adequate amount of sleep.

What counts as "adequate" differs from person to person. Some people need nine or more hours of sleep each night, while other people feel fine and refreshed with only six or seven. Anyone who says they don't need more than five hours of sleep is probably not functioning in life as well as they could be (or is sneaking naps on the side!).

In any case, children certainly need more sleep than adults. This is true of all mammalian species, not just humans. When we are first born, the healthy development of our brains requires much more sleep than when we are adults. No one knows exactly when dreaming begins, but we do know that the brain processes correlated with dreaming are highly active at the very beginning of life.

More than fifty years ago, scientists discovered that sleep is not a unitary state but actually involves many different stages of brain activity. When we go to sleep at night our brains do not simply shut down, like turning off a light switch. On the contrary, the brains of humans and nearly all other mammals pass through several cycles of complex activation during the night. The most energetic stage is known as "rapid eye movement" sleep, or REM sleep, and it alternates with several other stages known collectively as non-REM sleep. In REM sleep the brain becomes amazingly active, sometimes even more active than it is during the waking state. Whereas non-REM sleep is relatively quiet and low-energy,

REM sleep cranks up the neural volume in many parts of the brain.

For all mammals, the beginning of life is when they experience the highest proportion of REM sleep. From mice to elephants, from cats to whales, the newborns of virtually every mammalian species have much more REM sleep than adults do. Human babies spend up to 80 percent of their sleep in REM, compared to approximately 25 percent in human adults. This is a remarkable fact that indicates a close relationship between REM sleep and the growth of the brain. Even more remarkably, the high proportion of REM sleep starts before birth, in the womb. Human fetuses toward the end of pregnancy are also going through regular cycles of waking, REM sleep, and non-REM sleep, with a marked emphasis on the REM stage. These findings tell us that REM sleep serves an adaptive function in the growth and maturation of the mammalian brain. Although researchers continue to debate the nature of this function, it clearly involves the complicated but essential task of wiring all the neural connections necessary for the full development of our mental abilities.

Many studies have shown that REM sleep is closely connected to dreaming. It would be too simplistic to say that REM sleep is *identical* to dreaming. People can have dreams with no REM sleep and REM sleep with no dreams. But the neuroscientific evidence does indicate that the brain activities of REM sleep are a regular *trigger* for dreaming. We do not know if newborns or fetuses in the womb are actually dreaming, but we do know their brains are spending a large proportion of their time in the stage of sleep most often associated with dreams. If they are not dreaming, they are certainly getting ready to dream.

At the cutting edge of neuroscientific research, researchers are identifying the areas of the brain that seem to play an especially big role in REM sleep. One of these areas is called the limbic system. It underlies our instinctual behavior patterns (such as the fight-flight response) and our capacity to form long-term memories. Another brain area highly active in REM sleep is the occipital lobe, where visual imagery is formed and processed. At the same time, REM sleep also involves diminished activity in the prefrontal cortex, which provides the neural foundation for linear thinking and rational awareness.

The picture revealed by this research seems entirely consistent with the personal experience of dreaming. REM sleep encourages less focus on rational thought and more on instincts, memories, and visual imagery. The implication is that dreaming is a natural expression of the brain's activities during sleep with deep roots in the evolution of all mammalian species.


## PLAY

Another key fact from evolution, and the fourth scientific research topic we will discuss, regards the central role of play in mammalian development. The younger members of nearly all mammalian species engage in games of "make-believe." They pretend to fight, hunt, chase, hide, mate, and nurture, all behaviors that will be necessary for survival in adulthood. By playing these kinds of games the young creatures are able to prepare for the challenges of later life in a safe environment, without worrying about the consequences of failure. As an adult it can be fatal to lose a fight, so pretend fighting in childhood gives creatures a chance to try out different strategies and rehearse adaptive behaviors that will increase the chances of success if and when they actually have to battle in later life.

In light of evolutionary research on play, we can understand dreaming as a kind of play, the play of the imagination in sleep. In dreams we enter a safe, make-believe environment in which we can test out different responses to situations related to our survival and growth. This is the idea behind the "threat simulation theory" of neuroscientist Antti Revonsuo. Revonsuo has argued that the high frequency of nightmares in childhood reflects an evolutionary adaptation that helps young humans prepare for the dangers they will likely face in the world. As we will see in later chapters, children often have nightmares about wild animals, strange men, and threatening natural forces like fire and water. These were the kinds of dangers our human ancestors typically encountered in their environment hundreds of thousands of years ago. Revonsuo says that children's nightmares "play" with these dangers by simulating their occurrence and rehearsing possible responses.

Not all children's nightmares can be explained in this way, but we believe Revonsuo's theory is very helpful in highlighting the genetically programmed tendency of the human brain to play in sleep—to dream creatively about our waking life concerns and to use the vast powers of our imaginations to anticipate and prepare for the challenges of adult life. Jung's notion of the prospective function of dreaming fits very well with Revonsuo's threat simulation theory, adding more evidence to support the compatibility of Jungian psychology and contemporary neuroscience.

## EMOTION

One of the more surprising results of brain research is the importance of emotion to rational thought. For ages philosophers, theologians, and scientists have asserted a fundamental split between reason and emotion: You cannot be rational if you are influenced by emotions. To develop your powers of reasoning, you must suppress or eliminate your emotions. This assumption turns out to be wrong. Neuroscientists have found that emotions are actually sophisticated expressions of mental analysis and evaluation. Without emotional input our reasoning faculties are severely diminished. There is no sharp split between the reasoning and feeling parts of the brain. Everything we perceive, think, and experience passes through an emotional filter that helps us assess the importance of what's happening and how we should respond to it. Obviously too much emotion can cloud reason, but trying to eliminate emotion does not make a person more rational or successful in life. Reason cannot function in a normal, healthy fashion without the active and continuous input of emotional information.

We see a direct relevance to children's dreaming in this research because dreams so often have strong emotional content that "carries over" into waking consciousness. A child wakes up from a scary dream of being chased by a wolf, and even though the image of the wolf is gone, the heart-pounding terror remains vividly in the child's mind. The emotional intensity of dreaming used to be taken as a sign of its irrationality, but now, thanks to current brain research, we can appreciate how the strong emotions that emerge in dreams are expressions of a deep kind of wisdom that can enhance the powers of waking consciousness. Much has been made in recent years about the importance of "emotional intelligence" in early child education. We believe there can be no more powerful way of boosting emotional intelligence in children (and adults too!) than by paying greater attention to their dreams.


## METAPHOR

The work of cognitive linguists George Lakoff and Mark Johnson has shown that our minds make sense of the world by using knowledge from one realm of experience to explore other realms we do not know as well. Metaphors in this perspective are not simply figures of speech but the basic building blocks of understanding. They pervade our thought, language, and reasoning, not just in art and poetry but in our everyday lives—and in our dreams, too.

The essence of metaphor is "understanding one kind of thing in terms of another." We use what we know to help us understand what we don't know. Metaphorical thinking comes naturally to us, thanks to the neocortex and its vast capacity for associating different thoughts, feelings, and memories as a means to greater knowledge. The use of metaphors is one of the defining traits of our species, giving us tremendous flexibility in problem-solving when faced with novel circumstances.

The metaphor-making genius of the human imagination consists in its infinite ability to create novel extensions of preexisting ideas. This is precisely what happens so often in dreaming, when the imagination weaves rich tapestries of meaning out of both common and personal metaphors. Lakoff makes the connection clear:

> [D]reaming is a form of thought. Powerful dreams are forms of thought that express emotionally powerful content. Two of the main results of cognitive science are that most thought is unconscious and most thought makes use of conceptual metaphor. Dreams are also a form of unconscious thought that makes use of conceptual metaphor.

According to Lakoff the metaphors in dreams often revolve around strong emotional concerns, putting hard-to-define feelings into vivid images and experientially engrossing scenarios. Once we know about the brain-mind processes involved in generating metaphors, we can see past the apparently crazy and bizarre aspects of dreaming to recognize a much deeper level of neural creativity and meaning-making.

Lakoff says that many of Freud's dream interpretations make more sense when understood as translations of common metaphors in dreams. We believe the same is true of Jung's interpretations. Jung's approach to symbolism in dreams corresponds very closely to the research of cognitive scientists like Lakoff on metaphorical thinking. Dreaming takes full advantage of the symbol-making, metaphor-generating powers of the mind, leveraging knowledge from one domain to expand our understanding into new realms.

## RESEARCH ON THE CONTENT
## OF CHILDREN'S DREAMS

A number of good empirical studies have been performed in recent years looking at patterns in the content of children's dreams. More studies need to be done in this area, as in all areas of dream research generally, but we can point to some findings that provide a solid foundation for exploring children's dreams along the lines we are proposing.

The best scientific study so far of children's dreams was conducted by David Foulkes at the University of Wyoming in the 1970s. Foulkes's study focused on a total of forty-six children who slept in his sleep laboratory several nights a year for a five-year period, awakening them at different stages of the sleep cycle and asking about their dreams. His results covered children from three to fifteen years of age, with 2,711 sleep lab awakenings to build on. He found that the younger children remembered fewer dreams, with simpler, more static content, than the older children. The younger children were more likely to be passive observers rather than active participants in their dreams, something that shifted with the older children, whose dreams became more active and dynamic. Foulkes explained these results by saying the increasingly sophisticated characteristics of children's dreaming reflect the developmental trajectory of their minds. As children's minds become capable of more complex thinking, they become capable of more complex dreaming.

The laboratory setting of Foulkes's study makes it unlikely the children reported any big dreams. His findings make sense in relation to the ordinary course of children's dreaming, but it does not entirely account for the qualities of extraordinary dream experiences in childhood. In big dreams children seem to express cognitive abilities beyond those of their waking minds, as the following chapters show.

In an authoritative summary of content analysis research, *Finding Meaning in Dreams: A Quantitative Approach*, G. William Domhoff highlights the finding from several studies showing that children's dreams have a higher proportion of animal characters compared to adult dreams. Domhoff also points to studies showing a higher frequency in children's dreams of misfortunes, aggressive social interactions, and experiences of being the victim of an attack. The big dreams to be discussed in the following chapters will display all of these themes in vivid detail.

Kate Adams, an educational psychologist at Bishop Grosseteste University in the UK, has done research on aspects of children's dreams very close to our interests in this book. She interviewed ninety-four children between the ages of nine and eleven about dreams with connections to something "divine," however each child defined that notion. The children came from Christian, Muslim, and secular backgrounds, and from all these groups she gathered dream reports that reflected important personal concerns of the dreamer and a deep spiritual curiosity about basic existential questions of human life. Perhaps we should not be surprised when Adams mentions,

> Several children told me that I was the only person with whom they had shared their dream—parents, some said, were not interested or told them, "It was just your imagination." As a result, the children retreated into a world of silence until a researcher with a genuine interest came along.

In 2005 Kelly published a study with several colleagues on the earliest remembered dreams of childhood. The analysis focused on the data from personal interviews with eighty-five people about the first dreams they could ever remember having. The conclusion of that study is worth mentioning here:

> This study has shown that most adults are able to remember a particularly vivid dream from early childhood. These dreams

tend to be frightening nightmares, with a mix of realistic and fantasy elements. Threat simulations were the most frequent motif, followed by titanic [a term explained in chapter 5] and family dreams. About a quarter of the earliest remembered dreams were positive experiences in terms of fulfilling wishes, connecting with spiritual beings, or enabling the dreamer to fly. Our findings largely agree with those of Foulkes' and Domhoff's content analysis studies of children's dreams, though our data show a higher percentage of nightmares and a greater degree of creative imagination. Revonsuo's threat simulation theory receives strong support from our findings, as does Jung's notion of early childhood as a time of "big dreaming." Freud's wish-fulfillment theory receives less support, though some earliest remembered dreams definitely do include a wish-fulfilling dimension.

More recently, Kelly has been using word search methods to study a 2011 survey of 1,199 American children ages eight to eighteen who responded to an online survey (conducted by Harris Interactive) asking them to describe an especially memorable dream. The initial results indicate that, compared to typical patterns of adult dreams, these children's dreams have more references to family, animals, fantastic beings, happiness, sadness, and flying. Some of the dreams from this survey are discussed later in the book. Of the 1,199 children who were contacted for the survey, 622 gave an answer of at least twenty words in length. This survey comes from a demographically diverse group of American children, suggesting that at least half the children in the country can recall a highly memorable dream when asked.

All of these studies of dream content in children have their limits. Even adults have difficulty describing the elusive, multisensory qualities of their dreams. For children, their immature linguistic abilities make it that much harder to convey a full sense of their dream experiences. Still, taking these limitations into account, we believe the evidence from these studies presents a compelling picture of dreaming as a natural, normal part of healthy child development. We end this chapter with the same conclusion as in chapter 1, using current brain science instead of Jungian psychology: Children's dreaming emerges out of the core potentiality of their unconscious imaginations to promote greater mental flexibility, imaginative creativity, and adaptive problem-solving.

# 3

# DREAMS OF EARLY CHILDHOOD

Now we begin to explore a collection of actual children's dreams that we have gathered from a variety of sources. Some of the dreams come from people who are children now, and others come from adults recalling dreams from earlier in life. Some come from people we know personally and were able to ask follow-up questions, and others come from third-person sources in books and articles. A few come from people whose dreams were examined in Jung's seminars, while most come from our own investigations and interviews. We do not claim that these examples represent all possible types of big dreams in childhood. Undoubtedly some readers have experienced dreams that differed in various ways from the ones discussed here. Indeed, almost every dream has its own quirky, idiosyncratic details that make it slightly different from every other dream. This is one of the reasons why it's impossible to write a universal dictionary of dream symbols—the potential variations of dreaming experience are virtually infinite.

The next three chapters put into practice the basic principles of interpreting an unusually powerful dream from childhood, whether your own or someone else's. We have selected these dream reports because they illustrate archetypal themes we have found especially important and meaningful in children's psychological and spiritual development. We will not pursue every possible dimension of meaning in the dreams, instead limiting ourselves to discoveries that (a) relate to collective human experience and (b) can be reached fairly quickly and easily—the low-hanging fruit, you might say. Once you become comfortable working with children's dreams at this level, you can explore other levels with more confidence and skill.

As mentioned in the previous chapter, the dreams of children in the three- to five-year-old range tend to be very brief in length, with few characters (mostly family members, animals, friends, and fantasy figures), little action, and minimal plot. The settings tend to be home or homelike. The child often takes the perspective of a passive observer watching a series of images. This seems to be the typical profile of "little" dreams in early childhood.

When a preschool child has a big dream it may still display some of those features, but the archetypal energy transforms it into something much more impactful and dramatic, an experience they might remember for a lifetime. Such dreams are rare, but when they occur they can change the way the young child looks at the world.

For each dream we will provide the dream report as described by the dreamer, with a title we have chosen to make it easy for readers to remember. In most cases we have used pseudonyms to preserve the privacy of the individuals who shared their dreams with us. We start by analyzing each dream in terms of Jung's four-part dramatic structure, and then we explore some of its archetypal themes and connections to the science of brain development. We end each discussion not with definitive answers but with pragmatic reflections and open-ended questions.

## THE ENCHANTED AQUARIUM

### "Sam"

*I had this dream when I was about four years old. My parents were into sea life so in addition to taking us to Marine World they also took us to the aquarium. In my dream my dad is towering over me. I am with him at the aquarium along with two other kids from my preschool. Dad picks me up and puts me on his shoulders. I looked into the tank of the lion fish. Then I look at the dolphin tank. I see "Buster" the dolphin* [a well-known attraction at the aquarium]. *I realize in the dream that the air is like water. I feel a sense of weightlessness. I go around swimming up the stairwell and hovering there. It was a very enchanted feeling I woke up with.*

*Locale:* The aquarium, an enjoyable and educational space he associates with his parents. The time is present day. The characters include Sam, his dad, the two preschool children, the lion fish, and Buster the dolphin.

*Exposition:* Sam is looking up at his father's towering figure.

*Peripeteia:* His father picks him up. Sam looks at the fish in the aquarium, then he becomes like a fish, weightless, swimming through the air, rising upward.

*Lysis:* Hovering above the others.

In many ways this is a fairly typical preschool-age dream, with a brief plot, little action, just a few characters, and some animals. But several features of this dream indicate its archetypal power and potential, beyond the fact it was so clear and vivid that Sam remembered it more than twenty years later.

The upward movement in the dream stands out as a central theme. Sam starts with a view looking up at his father "towering" over him. This perspective emphasizes how small Sam is, how far below his father he stands. At one level this is a natural recognition of Sam's actual size in waking life compared to his father. An up-down contrast like this also reflects an archetypal yearning for growth, a prospective awareness of where his development is leading him. Sam is looking up at his own future potential for becoming a mature adult like his dad. He may not consciously grasp that idea yet, but the exposition of his dream sets him in a relationship with his father defined by their different sizes—a difference that Sam's physical and psychological growth will eventually overcome.

Sam's first move upward comes from his father lifting him up, above his preschool classmates, to an elevated perspective where the fish become visible to him. As a child Sam had a good relationship with his father, so this image seems like an accurate metaphor of his father's efforts to "raise" Sam well, to help him "grow up." People sometimes speak of "standing on the shoulders of giants," a saying that Sam's dream embodies in the physical metaphor of actually standing on his father's shoulders.

From this higher perspective Sam notices the creatures in the aquarium tanks. First is the "lion fish," a species whose name combines notions of sea and land. Then he sees the dolphin named "Buster," a sea-dwelling mammal who has become a part of the local human community.

This is a good time to point out that when dreams include very specific details like the names of these two animals observed by Sam, it's worth paying attention to their distinctive qualities. As we have said earlier, the dreaming imagination has infinite creativity at its disposal. It can put us at any time, in any place, with anyone, engaged in any kind of activity. So when a dream goes to the trouble of focusing awareness on very particular details, we should consider what those details are adding to the dream's overall story and impact.

Here, Sam's dream focuses on two specific aquarium creatures who are hybrids, crossing zoological boundaries and combining the qualities of radically different forms of life. There may be other connections between the lion fish and Buster the dolphin, but one is certainly their hybrid nature.

This is significant because immediately after seeing them Sam has the magical, boundary-crossing realization that the air is like the water, and he's basically in the same medium as the lion fish and dolphin. Up to this point the dream has portrayed a realistic scenario, the kind of thing that might actually happen in waking life. Here, though, Sam's awareness shifts away from ordinary physical reality to a new reality mixing elements that are normally separated. His sense of gravity lightens and he is able to rise upward beyond his father's shoulders into the stairwell of the aquarium.

Religious traditions all over the world have spoken of magical ascents that revealed mystical insights into divine reality. In the Book of Genesis, Jacob has a dream of a ladder reaching to heaven that helps reassure him of his connection to God. In the Qur'an the Muslim prophet Muhammad describes a fantastic "Night Journey" in which he flies upward to receive special teachings from Allah. Stories about the Tibetan Buddhist sage Milarepa say that he gained the power to fly and soar through the celestial realms. Whether or not these religious stories are factually true, they do express an archetypal truth about the human yearning for "higher" knowledge—knowledge beyond what we currently understand, knowledge that crosses normal boundaries and connects us to the beneficial, life-affirming energies of creation.

Sam's dream taps into this archetypal theme. His dream reveals a classic mystical insight in a language relevant to a four-year-old's life experiences. He recognizes a cross-species kinship with other forms of life and discovers his own ability to shift his awareness upward in a way that seems impossible from an ordinary human perspective.

Other lines of meaning in the dream flow from this one. In terms of Sam's relationship with his father, the dream imagines rising past his dad so that Sam is the one towering above everyone else. In this book we do not often refer to the ideas of Sigmund Freud, but here is a good case illustrating the oedipal dynamic between fathers and sons. To use Jung's language, this was an archetypal theme for Freud, reflecting a deeply instinctive pattern of relationship in human families. Sam's dream takes a nonviolent approach to the relationship, not fighting against his father as in Freud's theory but rather using his dad's support as a springboard for higher development.

The theme of being able to breathe in water calls forth other symbolic possibilities that carry archetypal significance. One has to do with the beginning of every human life in the watery uterine environment of the mother's womb. We all start life with the ability to breathe in water, and something of that awareness may linger in Sam's unconscious, emerging in this dream. Perhaps that unconscious knowledge goes farther back, into the evolutionary history of all earthly life as it first developed underwater, in the primordial oceans of our planet. As a four-year-old Sam couldn't possibly "know" any of this in a rational way. But his big dream planted the seeds of these archetypal insights so vividly in his mind that he has remembered them for the rest of his life.

The lysis of the dream suggests a future challenge for Sam. His report ends with him hovering high up in the stairwell—aloft and free, but unconnected to others and distant from the ground. The dream thus concludes on a note of suspended awareness, which raises the question of whether Sam can find new connections in this higher realm of insight. This, too, is a frequent theme of mystical literature, the tension between pursuing heavenly revelations and nurturing intimate relationships here on earth. To strive for an awareness of higher truths is often to become separated from one's community. Sam's dream provides an inspiring vision of his own potential growth and a cautionary insight about difficulties he may face in the future.

### THE BUNNY I LEFT BEHIND

#### "Brenda"

*My family (there were people with me and it had the feeling of my family although I never saw their faces) was at home (but it really was not our house in the dream). The house was on fire. Flames were shooting up around things but not burning them. We had to exit the house from the upstairs. I had to leave my beloved stuffed bunny on the couch. I could have easily saved him but I did not. I was not afraid of the fire. It was upsetting to me to have to leave the bunny. (This dream was recurring.)*

*Locale:* A place that feels like home, but is not the physical structure where she and her family live. The time seems to be the present. The characters are a vague collection of her family and her stuffed bunny.

   *Exposition:* Her home is on fire.

   *Peripeteia:* She and her family flee the fire.

   *Lysis:* She leaves her stuffed bunny behind.

Brenda said she was about four when she started experiencing this dream, which contains many of the typical details of dreams in preschool-age children. The plot was brief, the setting home-like, the characters familiar. Yet despite its simplicity, Brenda's dream made a powerful impact on her imagination. She could remember it very clearly more than forty years later, when she told it to us.

   The recurrence of the dream certainly accounts for a large part of its memorability. When a dream comes more than once, it nearly always signals an urgent concern coming from the unconscious mind, a concern about something that holds special significance for the individual's waking life. Many of the big dreams we discuss in this book are recurrent, with each new instance reinforcing the emotional impact of the underlying archetypal theme.

   Brenda's dream starts with a strange ambiguity about her setting and companions. She is at home, but not exactly her current house. She is with her family, but she can't see their faces. When dreams have vague uncertainties like this, it can indicate a shift in the individual's awareness from present day to archetypal realities. Brenda's recurrent dreams were not just about her personal home and family; they were also about the collective human experience of homes and families.

   That archetypal home is on fire. We will discuss fire, an important theme in children's big dreams, in more detail in chapter 5. Here, we focus on Brenda's perspective on the fire as a source of danger and destruction. This might indicate emotional problems at home, although Brenda said she had a good, nontraumatic childhood. The dream is silent about who or what set the fire;

the flames just start, quickly consuming her home and threatening her family. Strangely, she says the fire doesn't scare her; it endangers everything and everyone else, but she does not fear it. Why not?

Perhaps because she knows at an unconscious level how quickly she is growing up. She knows she will survive the rising flames because they reflect her own rising development. The burning energy of fire is actually more than just a metaphor of growth. It literally expresses the accelerating chemical dynamics of that physical growth in the child's metabolism and neurological development. Like Sam, her dream is a prospective vision of where that growth is leading her.

The odd detail about escaping the fire by going upstairs fits with our interpretation because it emphasizes the same kind of upward movement we saw in Sam's dream. The fiery pace of Brenda's growth will eventually destroy her early childhood life as she rises up to become her future self.

A distinctive feature of Brenda's recurrent dreams is that they focus not on where she is going, but on what she must leave behind, namely, her stuffed bunny. As any parent knows, a child's stuffed animal can become the object of intense emotional attachment. By playing with such beloved figures children explore the complicated world of interpersonal relationships and practice various kinds of social behavior in a safe, emotionally manageable space. In Brenda's dreams her stuffed bunny seems to metaphorically represent her own early childhood, conveying a message that to grow up she must leave the bunny behind.

The bunny also embodies her emerging capacity to mourn, to accept experiences of loss, feelings of sadness, and the inevitability of change. Brenda could have gone back to save her bunny, but she chose not to do so. In that poignant moment, which her dreams repeated again and again for extra emotional emphasis, Brenda confronted a deep existential truth about human life: We can't go back. To enter a new developmental stage is to leave an old stage behind. Brenda's dream prepared her for the impending loss of early childhood and taught her about the creative destruction at the fiery core of human growth.

## THE WAYFARER'S CHURCH

### *"Brian"*

*I am walking along a lane. The lane is long, long and straight, stretching into the distance, with fields on either side. The sun is low and red, round like a fireball, for the day is nearing sunset. I know I have a long way to go.*

*As I proceed, I see two people in the distance, standing in the middle of the lane. They are dressed in black; their clothes are stiff and old-fashioned, belonging to another age. I approach with some apprehension.*

*The couple are evidently man and wife. They are waiting by the entrance to a church, which stands by the left of the lane.*

*The church is clear in the dream, with a square tower, after the manner of many Norfolk churches. There are three arched windows, filled with stained glass, in the long wall of the nave. It stands at right angles to the lane, with its tower overlooking the roadway. I see no sign of a graveyard. The old man and woman appear friendly, and invite me into the grounds of the church. We enter from the far side.*

*Now it can be seen that the building is actually a ruin. The tower alone is intact. The body and roof of the church have collapsed, leaving only one wall standing—the long wall I saw as I approached. Using the fallen stone, a humble dwelling has been constructed—a cottage which utilizes the remaining wall as its rear wall. The couple live in this subordinate lay building.*

*They welcome me in. I am weary and untrusting.*

*As the cottage door swings open, I see within a bright fire burning and an aspect of homeliness.*

*Before I can cross the threshold, I wake up.*

*Locale:* A country road, and an old church. The time is indeterminate; it could be the present or far in the past. The only characters are the dreamer and the old married couple.

*Exposition:* He is walking down the road and encounters the old couple.

*Peripeteia:* He follows them to their dwelling inside the ruins of the church.

*Lysis:* He approaches but does not cross the threshold into their home.

"Brian" is Brian Aldiss, an award-winning British science fiction author who described this dream for a book edited by Nicholas Royle called *The Tiger Garden: A Book of Writers' Dreams* (1996). The writers, more than two hundred of them, were asked to relate a memorable dream, and many of them, like Aldiss, chose to describe big dreams from their childhood. Not surprisingly, the descriptions from this group of novelists and short-story authors can be quite detailed and even poetic, more so than we usually find in the dream reports of people who are not professional writers. That makes them an especially good source of insight into the creative subtleties of children's dreams.

Aldiss said he experienced this dream in the early spring of 1931, at the age of five. The setting is culturally familiar to him but does not seem to relate to any specific place in the world of his waking life. Again, the presence of anonymous characters and generic settings opens up the possibility of archetypal meanings. Young Brian finds himself in a kind of fairy tale: A child, alone on a country road, meets some strange old people and follows them into their home amid mysterious ruins. He describes a kind of ominous dread hanging over the scene, a feeling that intensifies as he goes deeper into the ruins and comes to the threshold of the old couple's home. The fire inside represents the warmth and radiance of their abode and their compassionate feelings toward him. But the structure itself seems fragile and tenuous, as if it were fighting a losing battle against time.

Aldiss referred to this as a "life dream." He said it was "more than a dream, a vision of the kind which helps to guide one's future." He may not use Jung's psychological language, but Aldiss is making the same basic observation about the power and lifelong impact of big dreams in childhood. He said he felt so moved by the dream he painted a picture of it after he woke up. He showed the picture to his mother, who proudly displayed it to the rest of the family and their friends. Her acceptance and celebration of his visionary dream must have planted an encouraging seed for him to pursue a life devoted to art and imagination.

At one level Aldiss interpreted the old couple as his parents who were blocking his path through life, trying to restrain him within the crumbled confines of their religious faith. The ruins of the church reminded him of the decline of Christianity in modern society and in his personal life. Yet paradoxically, the emotional tone of the dream was mostly positive. It "radiated consolation" and gave him a strong sense of comfort. We interpret this aspect of the dream as indicating the fall of traditional, institutional religion in his life and the possibility of connecting with an ancient but still-surviving realm of spiritual warmth and companionship.

This dream came many times after that first instance in childhood. The details changed over time, reflecting new experiences and new challenges in his life. Ultimately, however, he said the dream had no final interpretation. Rather, he came to see it as a "prodromic dream, the dream of one who has a long way to go . . ." The word "prodromic" means something that anticipates an attack or disease, which we believe is essentially synonymous with Jung's notion of the prospective function of dreaming.

The five-year-old boy's dream highlights a fundamental tension in his growing consciousness, a tension that will recur in various forms throughout his life. Will he pursue his own path, or will he go back inside the ruins? Will he become lost in existential solitude, or will he find spiritual connection? The lysis of the dream leaves him right at the edge of decision, and thus provokes his waking mind to reflect on this emotionally charged moment at the threshold. It's like his own personal koan, an archetypal riddle he will ponder for a lifetime.

## THE ROBBER'S DEN

### "Gregor"

*All of a sudden I was in a dark robber's den that was lit only by a fire in a corner. A couple of figures sat around that fire. I especially noticed two robbers; one of them was very tall and strong, the other was a hop pole, thin as a rake, who laughed mischievously. I was hungry and asked for a piece of bread. The big one came toward me and scared me with curt words. Meantime the hop pole was slicing little pieces of clay of a big lump of clay that were given to me with a lazy smile. Both were standing beside me, until I had eaten the pieces of clay. I was really disgusted by it and woke up from it.*

*Locale:* Inside a robber's den. There is no sense of time. The only characters are the two robbers, one big and strong, the other thin and cunning.

*Exposition:* He is hungry and asks for food.

*Peripeteia:* The big robber speaks harshly to him, and the thin robber cuts him a piece of clay to eat.

*Lysis:* The dream ends with disgust after eating the clay.

This is one of the dreams presented by a student in Jung's seminar. It comes from an adult man who remembered it from when he was four or five years old, and like Brian Aldiss's dream it has a timeless, fairy-tale quality. It opens with the boy suddenly finding himself captive inside a robber's den, at the mercy of two strange men. This is a primordially dangerous situation, the stuff of nightmares for any child in any culture or period of history. We often hear children describe highly distressing dreams of being kidnapped, lost, or separated from their families. This is a type of dream guaranteed to get the boy's conscious attention.

The dream emphasizes the polarity of the two men as complementary types of male identity, which Jung calls "power" and "ruse." As archetypal figures, they symbolize possible paths of development for the masculine ego. At one level they likely reflect the potentials in the boy's own personality, which is still in the early stages of formation. At another level the two robbers reflect the social reality he will likely face when he grows up. He will probably have to deal with men who behave in this way, using dominating strength or cruel deception to mistreat others. This realization may be disturbing, but it also prepares him to respond more effectively to these kinds of people when he encounters them in the future.

Once again we find a child's dream with fire in it. Here the fire establishes that the robbers consider this cave their home. There is a womb-like quality to the cave: It's a warm, hidden place where a young human is bound inside. The boy asks for food, and his request elicits a strong reaction from the robbers, both of whom are orally aggressive toward him (the big one speaking sharply, the thin one forcing him to eat clay). The clay is of course the strangest and most disturbing element in the dream. As a mixture of earth and water, clay represents a merging of the elements. Clay has the potential (after a long time in fire) to become a piece of ceramic, a creation of culture, which might symbolize the boy's potential to become a mature adult in his community.

But that lies far in the future. For now, the child must absorb a darker lesson. As Jung puts the dream's message, "It is hard to accept this earth. You really have to eat dust, it is disgusting." In developmental terms the boy needs to grasp this existential truth because otherwise he will retreat from the world and never want to leave the comfortable security of childhood. Jung goes on to say, "He is forced to eat the clay. He does this with great disgust, but he does do it: he swallows the barely digestible reality, into which he is growing."

This boy's dream reveals another archetypal dimension of human development at this stage of life, namely, a recognition that even though he is growing *up*, he must also grow *down*, down into the earth, into the disgusting mixture of dirt and water that gave rise to mortal life, and into which mortal life ultimately returns. "In concluding, we can say that the dream is an *adhoratio*, a warning, encouragement, that is, a preview of the world now unfolding, which approaches the boy and which he has to swallow in God's name."

## THE CASTLE AND THE KEY

### Ella

*There is a scary castle and a bad knight. The castle is high on a hill where there is a good knight and a bad knight. The Little Einsteins were locked up by the bad knight. I have a key which I give to the good knight and he frees the Little Einsteins. Then I am flying the rocket ship past a big monster.*

*Locale:* The setting is a frightening castle up on a hill. No time is specified. The characters include a bad knight and good knight, the "Little Einsteins" (heroes in one of her favorite cartoons), and a monster.

*Exposition:* The Little Einsteins are held captive by the bad knight.

*Peripeteia:* She brings a key to the good knight, enabling the rescue of the Little Einsteins.

*Lysis:* She is the pilot of a monster-eluding rocket.

Ella is our niece/granddaughter, and she had this dream when she was three years old. She woke up very scared and immediately described to her parents a detailed narrative more complex than any dream she had told them before.

It might seem that Ella's dream has done nothing more than replicate a cartoon adventure she recently saw. In fact, one of the

*Little Einsteins* episodes has a very similar plot, with two knights fighting and a magic key saving the day. But this cultural connection does not diminish the meaningfulness of her dream. On the contrary, it shows how a young child's imagination creates her own meanings by drawing on archetypal images in popular culture. The cartoons of today are like the fairy tales of ages past—enchanting stories for children that revolve around timeless themes such as the struggle between good and evil. Ella's dream takes the *Little Einsteins* episode and makes it her own adventure in which she can play an active role. Recall that young children's dreams tend to be passive, with little action or initiative. Here in Ella's dream she's right in the thick of the plot. She is the one who brings the special object that enables the good knight to release her beloved Little Einsteins characters.

In many indigenous cultures around the world, people dream of mythic characters and ancestral spirits that feature in commonly told stories. Anthropologists used to think these were somehow fake dreams, taken from cultural legends rather than personal dream experience. Recently, however, anthropologists have realized these experiences are just what the indigenous people said they are, namely, dreams in which mythological themes are woven into the individual's personal life story. Such dreams are authentic expressions of the human yearning to connect with a realm of power, goodness, and wisdom greater than oneself.

For Ella, the Little Einsteins are essentially mythic characters. Her dream creatively connects their cultural story with her personal life and growing abilities. The power of this connection and its stimulating effect on Ella's development can perhaps be seen in the lysis of the dream, the final image of the rocket ship and the monster. These elements were not part of the cartoon episode she saw; they are additions from her own imagination. They express another archetypal perspective on Ella's early life development. Fueled by her successful actions in liberating the Little Einsteins, she is growing with all the speed and power of a rocket, but she knows that monsters are still out there, threatening her and those whom she cares about.

## MY GOOD MONSTER ANGEL

### *"Alexi"*

*I had many nightmares of being chased by either wolves or monsters from a meadow area behind my home. Each time it was similar. When I got home I would either hide in my bedroom or in my bathroom. Although, before I go into either room, I was safe behind the main front door. Once I got into either room, the wolf or monster was able to get in, but not into the bedroom or bathroom. If I were to hide under the bed behind the overhanging sheet or in the shower stall behind the shower curtain, the wolf or monster would be able to get beyond the door but not under the sheet or behind the curtain. In the final dream I went into my aunt's high window, leaped like a deer, spoke with her in her kitchen and ran out the front door. I ran across to my home, into my bedroom window, a similar leap as both windows were high from the ground. As I looked back, I saw the monster do a similar leap into my aunt's and out following me. I hid crouched under the window between my brother's and my beds. My cousin and younger brother were playing at the foot of the beds. The monster came in, spoke to them, telling them he had killed everyone in the world and my family and close friends were next. He left. I then summoned my Good Monster/Angel and told him what had happened. Later that night while I was (still in the dream) asleep at home, they met in my parents' living room in a major confrontation. They fought and fought for what seemed a lifetime. I watched for a while from the corner of the hallway. Finally, before morning, my Good Monster/Angel (all in white; the Dark Monster was darkly dressed) came to me as I sat up in bed. He stood at my bedroom door, then he told me he had killed the Dark Monster and all the people he had killed were now safe, as were my family and friends.*

*Locale:* The dream moves in and out of his childhood home. The setting is realistic and familiar. The characters are the wolf or monster, his aunt, his cousin and younger brother, other family and close friends, and his "Good Monster/Angel."

*Exposition:* The wolf or monster comes from the meadow behind his house and chases him.

*Peripeteia:* He flees, hides, and overhears the monster saying he killed Alexi's family, friends, and the whole world. Alexi beckons his Good Monster/Angel, who fights the monster in epic combat.

*Lysis:* The Good Monster defeats the Dark Monster, and all his family and friends are restored to life.

Alexi had this dream when he was four, and he can still remember it vividly many decades later. It's longer than most early childhood dreams, although many chasing nightmares have this very quality of feeling trapped in an endless pursuit and conflict. Unlike the other dreams we have looked at, this one sets Alexi in the familiar details of his actual waking-life home. This is where he and his family live, yet this normally safe space has been invaded by a violent outside force that he cannot escape.

The emphasis throughout the first part of the dream is on Alexi's inability to escape the wolf or monster (an ambiguity that can indicate the presence of archetypal energy). No matter what he does, no matter how fast he runs or how high he leaps, no matter where he hides, the "Dark Monster" can follow and find him. The genocidal power of this evil creature, its antagonism toward all human life, has found its way into this four-year-old boy's dreaming imagination. Alexi is trapped by this monstrous force of death and destruction, unable to fight or flee, powerless.

At this moment Alexi does something unexpected—he looks outside himself, outside the boundaries of his ordinary life, and summons a mythic power of his own, a power that will fight on his behalf. It's a monster, but a good monster. He also refers to it as an angel, a benevolent supernatural being who protects humans and connects them to the divine. The Good Monster/Angel serves as a kind of therapist or confessor to Alexi, listening to his story of the Dark Monster's horrible deeds.

Then comes another surprising turn in the plot: Alexi goes to sleep. After talking to the Good Monster/Angel, the scene shifts in time to later that night, when Alexi is sleeping. The Good Monster/Angel and the Dark Monster meet in combat, and it's not clear whether he's awake or dreaming, but Alexi observes this titanic battle for what seems like a lifetime. Indeed, the battle between good and evil never ends; it grips us throughout our lives. In that sense the dream is an accurate prospective insight into the eternal moral struggles of human existence. Alexi's inability to escape the monster is reframed as a timeless archetypal conflict between the forces of life and death.

When people experience dreams within dreams, it usually indicates a deepening of awareness, an opening into new realms of the unconscious mind. In Alexi's dream this dream-within-a-dream emphasizes the profound significance of what's being revealed to him. He is witnessing a cosmic clash that threatens to consume his home, his family, and the whole human world.

The dream's lysis brings the final surprise of a happy ending. The Good Monster/Angel wins, the Dark Monster loses. All of Alexi's family and friends are restored to life. This might seem naïve and overly optimistic, like a Freudian wish fulfillment. We feel it can also be interpreted as an expression of basic trust and hope in the cause of life. In this terrifying dream Alexi must accept the inescapable power of death, yet he also gains a vision of the triumphant power of life, an inspiring vision that he has carried in his mind ever since.

## THE BLUE SNAIL

### "Helen"

*My first dream was the image of a blue snail. I have remembered it my whole life.*

*Locale:* No setting or time. The snail is the only character.
*Exposition:* She sees an image of a blue snail.

*Peripeteia:* There is no action or plot, just the image.
*Lysis:* It ends as it begins.

We first mentioned Helen's dream in the introduction. She was around five years old when she had the dream, and she told it to us at the age of ninety-five—ninety years later! There may have been more to the dream in terms of characters and actions, none of which has remained in her memory. What did remain was this peculiar image of a blue snail. She had no idea why the dream came to her or what it meant; she just knew it had always stayed in her mind.

Many other dreams discussed in this chapter touch on the question of what home means for a growing child. In light of that theme, perhaps we could see the snail in Helen's dream as a creature with the distinctive feature of carrying its home on its back. In this sense, a snail embodies the union of home and independence. As we found with other children's dreams, the experience of growing away from home and toward independence is both exciting and frightening. For children at this developmental stage, a snail might be a good symbol of a future integration of these two important values in human life.

Helen offered no associations to the color blue. We could speculate about blue being a stereotypically "boy" color, or the color of sadness, or the color of the ocean, and so on, and play out lines of interpretation that might be relevant to Helen's life. But that discussion might distract attention from the visceral impact of the dream, which was to generate a lifelong sense of wonder in Helen. Starting at the age of five she knew there is more to the world than meets the waking eye. She became more prepared for things that might appear strange or bizarre. She discovered the spontaneous whimsy of her own imagination. The vivid memory of the blue snail carried these insights from early childhood throughout the course of her life.

The big dreams of very young children push their minds in new directions, giving them glimpses of realities, truths, and paradoxes that will shape their later development. This accounts for some of the fear that accompanies these dreams—a natural fear of the unknown. The best thing a parent can do is help ease children's fears about the strangeness of these dreams. Children take their cues from their parents, so if you don't treat dreams as bizarre and meaningless, your children won't either. Once you have reassured a child that it is okay to have weird dreams, once they feel safe and confident they won't be ridiculed or judged for admitting and talking about such odd experiences, then you can ask some of the questions we have suggested here, looking more closely at the settings and characters, exploring the most unusual elements, and considering how the dream ends (or doesn't end). It is important to remember that these conversations should extend only as long as the child feels comfortable. Sometimes children enjoy talking at length about their dreams, and at other times they show no interest at all. Children do not need an elaborate, methodical, adult-level analysis to benefit from their dreams. What they need from parents and other adult caregivers is a safe, respectful, welcoming space in which they can reflect on the creative expressions of their own nocturnal imaginations.

# 4

# DREAMS OF MIDDLE CHILDHOOD

By the age of five, most children have entered into some kind of formal system of schooling. It may not be their first experience with school (some children go to preschool from a very early age), and it may not even involve leaving the house to go to an institutional school at all (e.g., for children who are homeschooled). But around this age children's minds make a big developmental leap. They become capable of learning the basic cognitive skills of civilized life, such as reading, writing, and mathematics. They become aware of a wider social world, with different people, places, and ways of behaving. Just as important at this age is children's developmental leap in emotional intelligence. They are rapidly expanding their awareness of their own emotions and the emotions of others, giving them the ability to be more empathetic, cooperative, and effective in resolving social conflicts. Freud put great emphasis on this age as a crucial time when children's egos gain a new level of control over their unconscious instincts. Jung generally agreed with that view of child psychology, and so do we. The transition from early to middle childhood is marked by a much stronger capacity for self-directed action and abstract mental processing.

All of these changes influence the dynamics of dreaming. From the age of five onward, children's dreams tend to become more complex in form and content. The reports get longer and more detailed, with increasing physical activity and narrative sophistication and a wider range of settings and characters. The cultural references become more specific, nuanced, and thought-provoking. The dreamer's perspective shifts into an even greater variety of multidimensional forms. Middle childhood is an exciting time of dreaming possibility that opens up new horizons of growth, discovery, and archetypal wisdom.

## TWO SAMURAI WARRIORS

### "Ann Marie"

*I am in the side yard near the back corner of my childhood home. I see two patios up ahead. On the far right patio I see two elaborately dressed samurai warriors sword fighting. I think one of them is me. The two warriors are wearing ornamentation. It is daylight in the dream and all images are clear. We are dressed in beautiful silk oriental robes. One warrior's robe is blue with white designs and undergarments and the other's robe is red with white designs and white undergarments. We each carry large swords and display martial arts techniques, good mental abilities, and the characteristics of a master. While engaging in combat, neither could defeat the other, yet they fought.*

*Locale:* In the backyard of her childhood home, in the present. The two samurai are the only characters, and Ann Marie identifies herself in some way with one of them.

*Exposition:* She sees the two warriors in combat.

*Peripeteia:* She becomes one of the warriors, and the battle becomes more precise and skilled.

*Lysis:* None. The balance of forces is even, and the fighting goes on.

Ann Marie had this dream when she was early in grade school. In its portrayal of an epic battle between mighty opponents, it has a similar theme to some of the dreams reported by younger children in the previous chapter. Here, though, the details have taken on a new level of cultural sophistication, allowing for a wider variety of meanings to emerge.

Ann Marie did not have happy associations with her home environment in childhood, so the setting of the dream is not necessarily a source of comfort or security, as we might typically assume. On the contrary, she remembers home as being a dark and frightening place. Yet the dream does not convey a sense of violence or danger. Even though the characters are fighting in an ominous location, Ann Marie did not experience this as a scary dream. Given the high frequency of nightmares in childhood, it's worth paying attention to those dreams that *seem* like nightmares but are not experienced by the child as emotionally negative. It may be a sign the child has learned to maintain emotional balance and ego integrity during a tumultuous time of growth and change.

This seems to be the case with Ann Marie. The samurai warriors embody the virtues of self-control, precision, and beauty in the midst of mortal danger. For a child whose primary developmental task was trying to survive in an emotionally hostile atmosphere, the samurai offered a living symbol of the potential to channel those aggressive energies and contain their destructive effects. The fact that Ann Marie was not scared by the fighting in her dream suggests she successfully tapped into their deep, time-honored strength.

The "otherness" of the samurai warriors adds to the archetypal power of their presence in her dream. Ann Marie's home was in a small town in the American Midwest, very far from Japan and Japanese culture. She could not find help in her local community, either psychologically or spiritually, so she had to reach outside the boundaries of her culture to discover resources for survival and future growth.

Ann Marie's point of view in the dream changes in peculiar ways. She is both observing the samurai and acting as one of them. In describing the dream she goes back and forth from the first person ("we each carry large swords") to the third person ("yet they fought"). The ability to have this kind of dual perspective in a dream marks a big developmental achievement for children, showing they can both act and be aware of acting, the basic cognitive skill required for self-reflection. Ann Marie said she had these kinds of dreams frequently as a child, which may reflect the adaptive value this kind of "higher awareness" provided for her during this troubled time of her life.

No strong associations came to Ann Marie regarding the colors in the dream. The sheer beauty of the warriors' outfits remained most vividly in her memory, a wondrous vision of aesthetic creativity that has stayed with her ever since. "Over the years this dream often comes to mind," she said, "and I think of it as a possible guide for my mission in life." It gave her a profound and lasting sense of inner strength: "No one to depend on except my inner self, a few friends and family, and God's intuitive voice. That is the samurai in me."

## I WAS DREAMING THAT I WAS SLEEPING

### "Hector"

*I was riding my bike and it was a sunny day. Then it started raining with thunder and lightning. I had to walk my bike home because I couldn't ride it in the rain. I came home and my parents were sleeping in their bed. I went to my bedroom and saw myself sleeping in my bed. Then I was dreaming that I was sleeping. I left the room and the dream started all over again from riding my bike. I felt weird.*

*Locale:* The setting begins someplace outside near his home, then moves into the house. The characters are his parents and himself.

*Exposition:* He is riding his bike on a sunny day.

*Peripeteia:* A storm hits and forces him to walk his bike back home. Inside he sees his parents asleep, and then he sees himself asleep and realizes he is dreaming.

*Lysis:* He loops back to the beginning of the dream.

Hector is a nine-year-old Hispanic boy who reported this dream on a survey that asked children to describe an especially memorable dream. We can't know if Hector will still remember the dream years into the future, but it certainly made a tangible impact on his present-day awareness. Like the big dreams of younger children, it touches on existential questions that humans have wondered about through the ages, questions with fascinating religious and philosophical overtones.

The opening of the dream sounds like an idyllic moment of middle childhood. Younger children generally cannot ride bikes by themselves, but school-age children can, and Hector's dream starts with him enjoying the privileges of this age-appropriate ability: mobility, independence, speed. Riding a bicycle is a big developmental achievement in terms of the physical skills necessary for keeping your balance. To be able to ride a bike means that your body has gained a powerful new sense of orientation and control. There's a saying that once you learn to ride a bike, you never forget. It's a small but meaningful turning point from younger to middle childhood.

The sunny weather parallels the positive physical and psychological energy of his bike riding. Weather often appears in dreams as a symbolic aspect of outer nature (the environment, the elements) and also inner nature (emotions, the collective unconscious). In Hector's dream both dimensions seem to be in play. The sunny weather provides ideal environmental conditions and also mirrors the "sunny" enthusiasm that children generally experience cruising along on their bikes.

Then the weather changes, and Hector's dream takes a sharp turn in a darker direction. Humans instinctively react to sudden changes in the weather with alarm and wonder. When a storm suddenly hits it catches our attention, and we instantly shift into a threat-assessment mode of thought, trying to reorient in the new conditions and find a safe place to take shelter. A consequence of children getting old enough to set out on the road by themselves is that they become more vulnerable to such abrupt and dangerous shifts in the weather. What starts as a pleasantly sunny day suddenly turns into a raging thunderstorm. Here, Hector does not indicate any sense of personal danger from the storm, but he completely loses the power of riding his bicycle, and everything that goes with that. He has to use his feet again, and he has to go back home.

The primal forces of thunder, lightning, and rain have various symbolic shades of meaning and significance, not all of them negative. In Hector's dream the storm turns him away from a typical daytime activity and toward a realm of insight and knowledge that makes him feel "weird." The storm takes him out of a familiar setting and brings him to a place where his awareness shifts dramatically.

Ironically, this place of altered consciousness is his family home. Driven by the storm, Hector goes into the house and sees his parents asleep in bed. Freud would probably identify this image as a child's disguised fantasy of parental sexuality. That could be an accurate inference; most children by the age of nine have some idea about the birds and the bees, and it's natural for them to wonder what their parents do together in bed.

But the stronger emphasis of Hector's dream seems to be on the fact his parents are sleeping, just as he finds himself sleeping a moment later. His parents are unconscious, while he is conscious. He is aware of them, but they are not aware of him. He comes home from the storm with a new perspective that transcends that of his parents. He knows things they do not know.

Then the dream takes an even more dizzying turn: He encounters himself, sleeping in his bedroom. At this point Hector realizes he is dreaming of sleeping. His perspective now transcends not only his parents, but his own physical body. This moment of lucid self-awareness leads him back to the beginning of the dream, which starts over again in what seems like a recurrent loop (perhaps linked symbolically to the round wheels of his bicycle?). Hector's dream seems to have exposed him to a fundamental paradox of human consciousness: Once the process of self-reflection has begun, there is no end to the levels of awareness you may reach—and no way of knowing whether you are at the beginning or the end, the observer or the observed. Many people say they had lucid dreams frequently as children but then "lost" the ability when they grew up, and now they no longer have such dreams. However, a great deal of research has shown that many people experience lucid dreaming all the way through adulthood, so age is not the only factor. We do not know if Hector will continue having lucid dreams when he gets older, but his dreaming imagination has already shown a powerful capacity to provoke further developments of self-awareness. Like riding a bike, he will never forget he has this ability.

## THE TOY BUS

### "Richard"

*I had a toy bus and it got stuck under the fridge. I was crying and couldn't get the bus out.*

*Locale:* The setting is the kitchen of his home, a familiar place. He is the only character.
*Exposition:* He loses his toy bus under the refrigerator.
*Peripeteia:* He tries to get it out, but cannot do so.
*Lysis:* None. He is left crying.

Richard was seven or eight years old when he had this dream. He could still remember the scene forty years later, along with the feelings of frustration and sadness generated by this dream dilemma.

It's a very short dream, more like the reports from the pre-school children in the previous chapter. This may actually be a clue to one level of meaning in the dream: It brings Richard back to a conflict or problem from earlier in his life. Even though he is older now, the dream reminds him of unsettled concerns from a younger stage of his development.

No other characters appear in this dream, which is somewhat unusual in that most dreams have at least one other character besides the dreamer. If no other characters are present in a dream, we can be pretty sure it does not have to do with social relations, and we can be more confident it relates to fundamental concerns of each individual human being. Richard is facing this problem by himself, with no help from anyone else.

In a short dream it's especially important to look very carefully at the few details that do come through in the report. In Richard's dream, the toy bus is at the center of his attention, though he never actually sees it. A bus is something large, a motor vehicle that carries groups of people from one place to another (for example, a child from one school to another). A toy bus turns that large object into a small one, small enough for a child to play with. As with any toy, Richard's bus gives him the ability to interact with something big and powerful from the adult world, bringing it down to a scale he can manage. In this sense, toys are tools of perception that help children figure out how the world works.

In Richard's brief but very memorable dream, he loses his toy bus under the refrigerator. Here is another distinctive detail that bears consideration. Refrigerators tend to be large and prominent objects in most kitchens. They function to store food by keeping it cold. They can be associated in a positive sense to nutrition and preservation or, in a negative sense, to chilly emotions and hidden feelings. Richard's experience in the dream focuses on the formidable bulk of the refrigerator: It's too big for him to move; he is not strong enough to push it aside. The toy bus gave him the power to play with something bigger than himself, but now the refrigerator has taken that toy away, reminding Richard of his small size and physical weakness.

The lack of a lysis suggests the scenario of the dream does not represent a problem that can be "solved." Rather it highlights an archetypal situation that all humans eventually must confront: There are always bigger and stronger forces in life that can take away our most cherished possessions. This may seem like a grim message, but it's a truthful one, a piece of spiritual wisdom that many adults never fully appreciate. For a school-age child, such a dream provides a balancing perspective that keeps the growing ego from overestimating its strength and power. It's surely significant that Richard was raised as a Roman Catholic, a tradition that emphasizes the virtue of humility before God. As Richard grew up, this dream always stayed with him as a reminder of his limits (physical, psychological, spiritual) as a finite human being.

## THE GIRL OF THE RAINBOW

### "Inge"

*There was a beautiful rainbow rising just in front of me. I climbed up on it until I came into heaven. From there I called down to my friend Marietta that she should also come up. But she hesitated so long until the rainbow disintegrated and I fell down.*

*Locale:* A fantastic rainbow rising into heaven. Her friend Marietta is the one other character in addition to herself.

*Exposition:* She climbs the beautiful rainbow.

*Peripeteia:* She invites her friend to join the ascent, but her friend hesitates, and the upward motion is stalled.

*Lysis:* The rainbow disintegrates and the whole scene falls apart.

This dream was presented and analyzed by one of Jung's students, Dr. Emma Steiner, during his seminar. The dreamer was a six-year-old girl whose background was not further described (we have added the pseudonym "Inge"). Jung said this lack of personal information meant that nothing could be said about the *motivation* of the dream in relation to the girl's waking life. But it could still provide a good illustration of an *archetypal* theme in children's dreaming generally:

> We rather have to try to put ourselves in the typical situation of a six-year-old child to find out the various possibilities of such motivations; for we can notice that similar situations regularly produce similar motifs in dreams. This motif of an ascent to a magic world in particular can be found in numerous children's dreams. So we may probably assume that here we are dealing with a particularly typical problem of the infantile soul, as quite correctly indicated by Dr. Steiner. It is really a typical children's dream, coming from a typical children's situation.

As one would expect, Dr. Steiner and Jung explore and amplify the symbolism of the rainbow to heaven in great detail. All over the world, stories and myths about rainbows portray them as bridges between this world and something better, higher, more powerful, more divine. In the Book of Genesis the rainbow follows the flood as a sign of God's covenant to protect all life. In psychological terms the rainbow can express a child's ascent toward greater development and higher consciousness. From the perspective of evolutionary history, rainbows are one of the great natural sources for the experience of wonder. With their brilliant harmony of colors, their spontaneous and ephemeral beauty, and their sweeping geometric span across the sky, rainbows have always evoked feelings of awe and inspired visions of celestial realms beyond our earth-bound reality.

In Inge's dream her upward ascent on this magical bridge leads her to heaven, which would seem to be the ultimate goal. But once in heaven, Inge is still lacking something—she wants her friend Marietta to join her. Heaven may be wonderful, but Inge apparently feels it would be more wonderful if she could share it with a friend. Unfortunately the friend she invites, Marietta, "hesitates" in joining her, and with that loss of momentum the rainbow falls apart.

Dr. Steiner and Jung interpreted Marietta as a shadow figure symbolizing a part of Inge's unconscious mind that needs to be better integrated so that her development may continue in a positive direction. Jung emphasized that whenever a child rises to a new developmental stage, there is a danger of splitting off parts of the personality that have not developed as far or as fast, losing touch with important aspects of reality. Marietta can be seen as a split-off part of Inge's personality, a part that keeps her connected to the grounding reality of her social relations.

The lysis of the dream poses a challenge to Inge. If she is to continue her magical ascent along the path of healthy psychological development, she must stay connected to her friends, her social world, and everything that remains "below." She must find a way for those connections to extend across the rainbow bridge to join her in heaven. In the dream she takes the initiative to make contact with Marietta; she knows what she has to do, what she has to strive for. This is the kind of challenge that takes a lifetime to fulfill.

## THE KING'S RULE

### "Nancy"

*There were two people, a woman and a man, working on a train. Me and dad went on the train and we came back half naked. Dad and me ran home to tell my younger brother. Then we came outside to watch / be in a parade but it was a King and his soldiers instead. The King had a new rule starting today. If you have four people in your family you have to kill one of them and feed the meat to a Praying Mantis. There's this family that stayed at home, they moved to Canada. The new rule there: you can have four people in your family and the people who had to get killed were lined up by the King to write down names so he would know.*

*He sent soldiers to houses to find the people. The people waiting to die had to get water from the stream and they had to pee and poo in a ditch and they had to walk through it. The family in Canada was happy and they just had a new baby. Good ending.*

*Locale:* The settings include a train, her home, an outside area with a parade, and someplace in Canada. The characters are both familiar (her dad and brother) and unfamiliar (the man and woman, the King and his soldiers, the Canadian family, the people waiting to die), with a flesh-eating animal (the Praying Mantis).

*Exposition:* She and her dad are on a train.

*Peripeteia:* They go back home to her younger brother, and then hear a King's decree about killing the fourth member of every family. The perspective shifts to observing a family who is in, or escapes to, Canada. Other people suffer terribly from the King's rule.

*Lysis:* The family in Canada is happy, safe, and growing.

Nancy was six when she had this dream and told it to her mother, who shared it with us. Her younger brother was two years old at the time. The dream made a very strong impression on Nancy, and because her mother had always encouraged her to pay attention to her dreams Nancy felt comfortable describing it in as much detail as she could remember.

In the opening scene Nancy and her dad board a train operated by an unknown man and woman. They lose half their clothing when they get off, something that might suggest an oedipal fantasy. Whether or not that's the case, Nancy and her father seem to have learned something from their experience on the train, something they must urgently tell her younger brother, the fourth member of their family. It's only after they get home that the King's parade comes and the horrific rule is announced.

Nancy did not say as much, but the Praying Mantis in her dream must be monstrously large to feed on human flesh. Perhaps there's some meaning to the detail of "praying," as if this insect were connected to Nancy's perception of religion, but we can't be sure. What's clear in the dream is that a gruesome fate awaits the victims of the King's decree.

Who is the King? Nancy is old enough to know the country in which she lives, the United States, has never had a king. Her dream presents the King as an archetypal tyrant, a symbol of evil authority ruling over the social world. Because human development relies so heavily on social relations, we are vulnerable to grave danger when a single person gains control over the whole social environment. The King in Nancy's dream is a direct threat to her family. His rule means that someone in her family must die. The theme of a tyrannical king and his soldiers going through the land killing children recalls the biblical story of Herod and the baby Moses. It's a story that conveys both the terror of living in a tyrannical society and the hope of escaping to someplace better.

When Nancy's dream shifts to the Canadian scene, it opens a new way of looking at the problem. The dream looks outside her own cultural context (the United States) and envisions a different place where families of four can stay together. She does not dream of a perfect world, however. The King's decree means that many people will be executed after trudging through an excrement-filled ditch. It's an awful, hellish scene that Nancy observes but does not enter into. Rather than being consumed by horror and disgust, Nancy's awareness in the dream is able to stay with the Canadian family, who at the outset seems partly identified with her own family ("there's this family that stayed at home, they moved to Canada").

It might be too much to say the dream has a happy ending, but it does end on a positive emotional note. Her family has escaped the danger of the King's evil rule. In waking life Nancy's family was very close-knit, so her dream does not seem to reflect any actual separation of the family. Instead, the dream prompts an archetypal awareness of the fact that threats to one's family are always looming in the world. The pragmatic moral of her dream could be phrased like this: You have to be vigilant against people who try to act like "Kings" and control how your family lives and grows. Nancy had reached an age at which she could recognize both the promise and the perils of living in a wider social world. Her dream expresses this complex insight in terms of highly memorable images and feelings that her young mind can begin to process and carry with her through the course of her development.

## THE WATER WHEEL

### "Francine"

*I was a black man, about twenty years old. I remember clearly what I looked like, all the physical details: Tall, muscular, like an African-American, definitely not a black from East Africa. I was held on a wheel, a big one in wood. They had attached my wrists and ankles and I would sink into the water of a river, rolling into the water. (Sort of a mill wheel?) On the other side of the river there were people singing gospel, praying for me, other black people, my friends and my family, and probably others I did not know. A special voice, so beautiful and so pure, was the one I really remember. Although I was attached to the wheel and could not see the people on the other bank, I knew she was my mother, a big and powerful African woman. She looked tall, she had this "generous" breast and big arms made for hugs and cuddles. I knew I would die, everybody knew as well, they were singing for me to help alleviate my pain. I would wake up very sad, suffocating as if I still had water in my lungs, drowning.*

Locale: The dream is set on the banks of a river with connections to Africa. It could be any time. The dreamer imagines herself to be a radically different type of person—different in age, race, and gender. The other characters all seem to be dark-skinned as well, mostly family and friends, with the African mother standing out for the purity of her voice.

Exposition: The dreamer is bound to a wheel.

*Peripeteia:* The people sing for the dreamer, and he/she is able to distinguish the beautiful voice of her mother, as the wheel is rolled into the river.

*Lysis:* The dream ends with a sad recognition she is going to die, and a carry-over effect of constrained breathing and the sensation of drowning.

This was a recurring dream that started around the age of five and continued for many years. At first Francine told her mother about the dreams, but her mother became so disturbed and scared that Francine began pretending the dreams had stopped. To this day, more than thirty years later, Francine does not feel comfortable in or around water.

Needless to say, this is an unusual dream in many ways. It brings the awareness of a young white girl just growing up into the awareness of a twenty-year-old black man just about to die. Francine had no particular waking associations to this figure or the African setting, and we don't know any more details about the role of race and ethnicity in her life; if we did, we would likely find additional layers of meaning in this direction. Her dream transformation is more than just racial, though. She also changes her age, her gender, and her place in the life cycle. The dream radically expands her sphere of empathy, her capacity to see life through the eyes of others, to feel what it's like to be another person living in different circumstances.

No reason is given for the black man's punishment; the authorities never appear in the dream. The focus is on his suffering and imminent death. The specific means of his execution apparently involves binding him to a huge wooden wheel that will be rolled into a river, where he/Francine will drown. There is no thought of escape or resistance; a horrible, suffocating fate appears certain.

The downward pull of death is counterbalanced, however, by the beautiful singing of the family and friends gathered along the riverbank. Just as the wheel-rolling torment seems like a dramatic image of inescapable death, the gospel-singing black people seem like an equally dramatic image of consolation and spiritual comfort. If the dream is giving her an unusually vivid insight into the reality of death, it is also giving her an unusually strong awareness of the primal human connections that kindle in us the courage to keep living despite the sad knowledge of our finitude. The African mother, with her pure and beautiful voice, could not be a more perfect archetypal symbol of our ultimate family roots in the evolutionary history of our species. She reminds Francine that even in the moment of death she, the embodiment of all that is good and nurturing in human life, will be there to comfort and guide her wherever the wheel may lead.

Here again we find a dream that wrestles with deep questions far beyond the sphere of most children's ordinary waking lives. As always, there may be personal connections with recent events in Francine's waking life, TV shows she watched, people she knows, and so on. But when a dream goes to the trouble of creating such an otherworldly scenario, it's usually a sign that the meanings extend beyond the personal realm to archetypal issues and concerns. When children need to learn something about their waking-life families and friends, that's what they will dream about. When they need to learn something about the collective family of humankind, this is the kind of dream they will have. Francine, like all of us, is bound to a wheel of time rolling toward a certain end. Yet she, like all humans, remains connected to the uplifting power of her ancestral heritage, and her dream shows her that this spiritual lineage of life-affirming relationships will continue beyond her death.

## THE GOLDEN BICYCLE AND
## RIDING ON A SEA OF CATS

### "Ben"

*(Dream #1) I see a golden bicycle, with glowing golden light from behind. It's a ten-speed road bike, and it **glows**.*

*(Dream #2) I'm riding a bike, and the ground is covered with cats; it's like a sea of cats, cats as far as I can see; there are so many of them I can't see the ground beneath them. I'm worried about riding my bike on top of them, because they might get angry at me and attack me; and there are so many of them that if they did I'd be in real trouble. But then I notice that my bike's tires are made of soft, padded cotton gloves, like a ring of hands with the palms facing outwards; so when I ride over the cats they are patted and stroked by the gloves.*

(For the analysis we will consider the two dreams as one continuous dream.)

*Locale:* The settings are fantastic yet vague; there are no references to anything familiar or definite. The only characters are the sea of cats.

*Exposition:* He sees a glowing golden bicycle.

*Peripeteia:* He rides a bike across a vast gathering of cats, worrying he might hurt them and be attacked in response.

*Lysis:* He realizes his bike's tires are not hurting the cats but actually petting them.

Ben had these two dreams, one right after the other, between the ages of five and six. He had recently received a bike for his fifth birthday, and his family's cat had delivered a litter of kittens. As with Hector's dream earlier in this chapter, Ben's dream illustrates the important symbolic role that bicycles can play in school-age children's imaginations. The glowing, golden bicycle of the first dream is much bigger and more powerful than Ben's current bike, but it gives him a vision of what's possible, of where his growth is leading him. It's an image of supreme value, a treasured object to be fervently sought and longed for.

He realizes, however, that the freedom and power he enjoys on his bike brings a new realm of difficulty and danger. The sea of cats accurately reflected an aspect of his home in waking life, with kittens constantly underfoot and his parents warning him to be careful, especially on his bike. The dream extends this domestic situation to an all-consuming reality: Everywhere Ben looks, he sees cats. There is no avoiding them, no way of escaping the dilemma. His mounting anxiety stems from the conflict between his bike-riding energy and the safety of the smaller creatures underneath him. Can he grow stronger and faster without harming the lives that remain below?

In this sense, Ben's dream is similar to Inge's dream of the rainbow bridge. She tried and failed to stay connected to her friend Marietta, down below Inge's position in heaven. Ben is also "in heaven," riding his beloved bike, but he worries that the cats down below might attack him because his bicycle tires are hurting them. His connection to them is threatened by potential harm and violence. But unlike Inge, Ben finds a source of integration and harmony between the upper and lower energies. The magical tires of his bike have padded hands that touch the cats in a gentle and friendly way, not with the hurtful impact he feared. Together the two dreams gave Ben the confidence that he could enjoy the freedom and independence of his bicycle while still staying connected to the "lower" animal energies that are in danger of being split off by his rapid development in waking life.

Not all big dreams in childhood have a specific impact on the person's adult life, but this one did with Ben. As he grew older his fascination with bicycles became even stronger. Beginning at the age of seven he became a bike racer, and when he finished high school he took time off before college to create a small company that manufactured specially designed bicycle brakes. After he graduated from college he went to work for a major bicycle manufacturer, doing research and development on the company's newest lines of bikes.

Ben's great vocation in life first emerged in his childhood dream of a golden bicycle, leading him into a career designing some of the world's most sophisticated, high-tech bicycles. The dramatic night vision of this child bore amazing fruit in the creative work of his adult life.

By the end of middle childhood we begin to see the interests and desires that will shape the rest of a person's life. Big dreams offer a wonderful window into these emerging qualities of a child's personality. Highly memorable dreams in childhood are highly memorable precisely because they open children to new levels of awareness of themselves and the world around them. In these kinds of dreams children gain their first glimpses of larger realities and bigger questions in life. They discover the frightening conflicts and mysterious paradoxes that loom ahead on the path of human development, and they also see inspiring visions of future integration and creative health. Children six years of age and older become capable of speaking more articulately about their inner experiences and more curious about their meanings, giving parents, teachers, and counselors a chance to learn more about these psychologically and spiritually transformative kinds of dreams.

# 5

# DREAMS OF LATE CHILDHOOD AND EARLY ADOLESCENCE

Age does not really matter to the collective unconscious. However old we may be, the same primal instincts that emerged at the beginning of life continue to motivate us and guide our waking behavior, through later childhood and adolescence and into adulthood. It's no exaggeration to say that at a fundamental level of our minds, we are all still preschoolers! The deepest potentials of our personality unfold continuously throughout our lives, more quickly in some areas of the mind, more slowly in others. When we reach a new stage of growth, we often encounter new versions of unresolved issues from previous stages and less developed parts of the mind. Human development involves many twists and turns, many times when two steps forward are followed by one step backward. That is why older children's dreams often reach back to themes from earlier in life and combine them with visions of what may come in their adolescent and adult future.

The approach of adolescence makes itself felt in children's dreams well before the actual onset of puberty. In keeping with what Jung called the prospective function, dreams in late childhood anticipate the dramatic changes ahead and prepare children to respond adaptively to the various possibilities they may encounter. These dreams may be frightening or emotionally disturbing, but as we have found with younger children's dreams, the fear can be a sign that the child's waking ego is being pushed to grow beyond its comfort zone into a new stage of psychological and spiritual development.

By any standard, adolescence is a time of tremendous up-heaval in children's lives. The stable sense of personal identity they had formed in early and middle childhood is abruptly overthrown by the rapid physical and hormonal changes in their bodies. What-ever they thought they *were*, they no longer *are*. The old I is being left behind, and a new I lies ahead.

In the course of all these disorienting transformations, chil-dren must negotiate a new relationship with the collective uncon-scious. The drives and desires of reproduction, hinted at earlier, now come strongly to the fore. Many of the big dreams of late childhood involve sexually themed images, symbols, and scenarios that give children some initial glimpses into this powerful realm of human experience. Children at this age are certainly thinking about sexual questions and wondering about their own romantic potentials and prospects. Even if children speak very little of such matters with their parents, their dreams may help them express emotionally honest thoughts, fears, and hopes about their future as reproductively mature human beings.

This is also an age when spiritual yearnings and experiences can open up new directions for growth toward health, integra-tion, and creativity in adulthood. Many of the world's religious traditions pay special attention to children's dreams as indicators of a special personal identity or life destiny. In some cultures the dreams of a child may be the first indication the child is called to be a shaman or tribal healer. Among the Sambia people of New Guinea, for example, the dreams of children are regularly exam-ined for indications that the spirits have chosen a future shaman. In other religious traditions, children are given specific instruc-tions for seeking out spiritually revelatory dreams. Many Native American cultures practice the ritual of the vision quest, in which an adolescent leaves the village and goes out into the wilderness to fast, pray, and sleep until a special dream occurs.

These traditional spiritual practices are based on a deep psy-chological wisdom. In every human culture, the transition from childhood to adulthood is difficult and fraught with danger. A young person must somehow develop a strong, stable identity that is personally authentic and capable of playing an active role as a constructive member of society. Dreaming offers a valuable resource for this developmental challenge by highlighting the archetypal tensions of human life and offering inspiring visions of integrative potential.

## THE FLOWER PLANET

### "Michael"

*There is a planet made entirely of flowers where I arrived in a Buck Rogers–style rocket ship and fell in love with a girl of my own age who bore a strong resemblance to my cousin, who later died.*

*Locale:* The dream is set on a fantastic planet made of flowers. The only character is the girl of his same age, though references are made to the adventure hero Buck Rogers and a cousin.

*Exposition:* He arrives at the planet.

*Peripeteia:* He falls in love with the girl.

*Lysis:* It ends with his observation of the resemblance of the girl and his cousin.

The dreamer is Michael Moorcock, a British science fiction and fantasy writer born in 1939. He had this and several other "very vivid dreams" around the age of twelve, and he could still remember this one clearly when he reported it in the *Tiger Garden* anthology in 2006.

For children approaching adolescence, the prospect of a romantic relationship may indeed seem like traveling through the stars to an alien world. Right away we can appreciate the impact such a dream might have on a budding young writer of fantastic, otherworldly stories. Like many other children of his time, he followed the adventures of Buck Rogers in comics, movies, and radio programs, all of which provided a strong cultural stimulus to his young imagination. The archetypal symbolism of a rocket ship is similar to that of a bicycle or other technologies of transportation. It expresses feelings of increasing speed, power, mobility, autonomy, an expanded range of awareness and control—all of which accurately describe the developmental gains from late childhood into adolescence. Michael is riding a rocket ship of psychological and physiological growth on a journey steered by the evolution of our species and fueled by the archetypal energies surging up from the collective unconscious.

He arrives not at just any planet, but a planet made entirely of flowers. This whimsical image is actually a very accurate symbolic expression of where his developmental journey is leading. Flowers are the reproductive organs of plants and a widely used symbol for human sexuality, particularly in relation to women. There may not be any "real" planets made out of flowers, but twelve-year-old Michael is truly about to enter a stage of life in which flower-like beings fill the world of his awareness.

Once at the planet of flowers he meets a girl and falls in love with her. The mention of her being his same age seems to indicate an equality and mutuality between them. The two of them are a "good fit." She's like one of his cousins, so she's familiar, but she's *not* his cousin, so there's no moral barrier or taboo against a romance with her. The fairy-tale quality of the dream gives Michael an experiential sense of what it will feel like when he grows up and finds someone to love. The dream casts him as the hero of this magical adventure, like a Buck Rogers of romance.

The only cloud on this otherwise positive and inspiring dream is the later death of Michael's cousin. That detail was not part of the dream but came later in his description of it. Still, the association with her death seems to have colored Michael's memory of the original dream, giving it a tragic sense of premature loss. To discover love is to discover its fragility. A flower in blossom does not last forever.

## RATS INSIDE HER GOWN

### *"Megan"*

*I see a man dressed in black, in a black top hat with a cape. He is very mean. He has my sister. She is an adult, dressed as a dance hall girl. He says to her, "You will sleep with rats tonight!" Then rats start crawling inside her gown—I can see them moving!—I wake up very frightened!*

*Locale:* No specific setting is mentioned. The characters are a mean, black-clad man and her sister, who appears older. The dreamer observes rather than participates in the dream.

*Exposition:* The man has her sister in his control.

*Peripeteia:* The man commands that her sister will sleep with rats, and then rats are crawling underneath her clothes.

*Lysis:* She awakens in great fear.

Here is a much darker anticipation of reproductive maturity. This dream came to Megan earlier in childhood, around the age of seven, but it definitely looks ahead to the developmental issues and challenges that will arise in adolescence. She observes the action in the dream rather than participating in it, a common feature of younger children's dreams. But Megan is observing her older sister, a person very much like herself who is going through what she will go through in just a few years. Megan both observes and empathetically participates in the dream, and by the end she totally identifies with the emotional experience of her sister.

The man in black seems like a villain straight out of a cartoon. We can see in him archetypal elements of the shadow (split-off parts of the unconscious), male sexual aggression, and existential evil. Megan's sister is older in the dream, signaling the prospective nature of the scenario, as if it were saying, "This is what's coming." She is dressed in a way that symbolically relates to stereotypical ideas about sexually active young women. We don't know if this reflects the actual waking personality of Megan's sister, or an unconscious aspect of Megan herself, or the way men in her culture look at women generally. The conflict between Megan's sister and the man in black has many dimensions of potential meaning, all of which may be relevant at different times of her life. Herein lies one of the greatest gifts of big dreams in childhood—they offer a lifelong source of symbolic insight that helps us navigate through the many challenges of human development.

The visceral fear and intense memorability of this dream come from the detail of the rats getting underneath her sister's clothing. Megan's description suggests this was a vivid and terrifying image. The rats do the bidding of the man in black, and their malevolent connection seems appropriate given the generally negative cultural associations with rats as dirty, sneaky, aggressive vermin. The man in black extends his physical control over Megan's sister by setting the rats loose under her gown. Megan may or may not have been familiar with the sexual connotation of the phrase "to sleep with," but her dreaming imagination equates it with touching her under her clothes. In terms of archetypal symbolism, her dream could not be a clearer expression of a sadly realistic truth for girls approaching adolescence: There are rats and evil men out in the world who will try to force you to sleep with them. It might seem cruel to expose a young girl to such a grim reality, but the collective unconscious takes a more pragmatic approach. Forewarned is forearmed.

## THREE YOUNG WOMEN

### "William"

*I had a dream: From the street one could go down into a strange store. Richard and I went down. Three young women sat at a small table behind the counter. They gave us red sticks that we did not have to pay for: like sealing-wax that one could smoke. So we put them into our mouths and started to smoke. Then I staggered out of the store; I'd gotten all dizzy and sick.*

*Locale:* The setting is a strange subterranean store. The characters include a male friend and three young unfamiliar women.

*Exposition:* He and his friend go down into the store.

*Peripeteia:* The three young women give them red sticks to smoke.

*Lysis:* He leaves the store feeling disoriented and nauseous.

This dream was reported by a nine-year-old boy and presented during Jung's seminar by Dr. Markus Fierz. Even though the boy has not actually reached adolescence, his dream represents "an anticipation of puberty," in Jung's words. Like the two previous dreams considered in this chapter, William's dream looks ahead to his developmental future and the many-leveled transformations he will experience.

A male friend accompanies William, suggesting he is not the only person going through this process. They leave the ordinary daylight world of the street and go down into the ground, into an archetypal realm of mystery and magic. William calls it a "strange store," presumably meaning some kind of business where goods are kept, bought, and sold. As a symbol of the collective unconscious, the strange store is a place where William and his friend make contact with the archetypal powers of reproductive desire that will soon take on a driving importance in their waking lives.

These powers take the form of three young women, sitting at a table behind a counter. Their position indicates the store belongs to them. It is their place. They are the proprietors, the keepers of the goods, the arbiters of exchange. Jung and his students amplified this image of the three young women by referring to the three Fates of ancient Greek mythology, a group of shape-shifting, awe-inspiring women who guide the destiny of each human life. Jung also saw connections with the Holy Trinity of Christianity and the divine symbolism of the number three. We would add the three witches at the beginning of Shakespeare's play *Macbeth*, the "weird sisters" who accurately foretell Macbeth's future rise and fall.

The three women give William and his friend a very specific kind of object—red sticks made of sealing wax. William may have had personal associations to the sealing wax that could lead to other dimensions of meaning, but we can point out the ordinary function of sealing wax as a means of closing a letter or other form of personal communication. This suggests the sticks are somehow a means of sending a private message from the women to the boys. Sealing wax is also a substance that changes form when heated, echoing the theme of transformation, and the red color enhances the connection to fire, heat, and passion.

Unlike a normal store, no money is exchanged. The sticks are a gift from the three young women to William and his friend. The boys put this gift to their mouths and breathe in the smoke. No actual fire is mentioned, but the sticks function like cigarettes in transforming a substance outside the body into a substance that can travel inside the body. They complete the process of absorbing the women's gift into the boy's physical being.

In today's world many people may have negative associations with cigarette smoking, but in this dream the smoking seems to be symbolic of the changes these women are bringing into William's life. Jung said, "The boy is here being initiated, for the first time, into sexuality."

The smoke knocks him off balance and shifts his perception in unexpected ways. William's ego in the dream experiences this as unpleasant and nauseating, but as Jung pointed out, "what is disgusting is the unacceptable 'other'" that must be integrated into consciousness if a person is to develop a healthy and balanced personality. William returns to the level of the street a changed person, aware of feelings and sensations he never knew before.

## FALLING THROUGH THE CRACKS

### "Paul"

*I am always on a bridge and somehow my parents fall through the cracks in it. I would try to save them but could not reach them. (I would always wake up crying or at least quite disturbed.) There was always water under the bridge and the bridge was actually more like a California wharf than a bridge.*

*Locale:* The dream takes place on a bridge like a California wharf. His parents are the other characters.

*Exposition:* His parents fall through the cracks in the bridge.

*Peripeteia:* He tries to save them, but can't.

*Lysis:* He awakens crying and upset.

Paul shared this dream in a personal interview when he was eighty years old. He remembered the dream from when he was fourteen, growing up in Maine. It was a recurring dream that gave voice to complex feelings about the prospect of growing up and leaving his family. When adolescents grow up they gain new powers of independence, but at the same time they lose their "little child" connection with home and family. This adds a note of sadness and melancholy to adolescent development, and these mournful emotions often express themselves in dreaming.

The dream's setting was not fantastic or unrealistic, but it refers to a place far away from where Paul grew up. California, in the eyes of someone living on the East Coast of the United States in the 1940s, was a distant but alluring part of the country that would likely evoke cultural associations with gold, beaches, the wild west, and the fantasies of Hollywood. Paul had never visited California, but he had seen pictures and movies of it. His dream drew upon those images to set him in a place that's very different from his home, a land of future possibility and discovery. As a metaphor of adolescent development, the dream imagines Paul's coming growth in terms of a big geographic movement (like Michael's journey through space in the first dream of this chapter). It may also be significant that California lies to the west of Paul's home, in the direction of the sun's journey from dawn to dusk; this would add to the sense that he's moving through time in the dream.

We find it meaningful that Paul initially describes the structure as a bridge, and then refers to it as a California wharf. Both structures allow people to travel over bodies of water, but a bridge generally connects two sides of land, whereas a wharf simply stretches out over the water, then stops. A bridge preserves a two-way relationship, but a wharf leads in just one direction. That's where Paul is heading, out toward the ocean, beyond the land, beyond California, farther west into his life as a mature adult.

And sadly, his parents can't go with him. Paul can walk on the bridge/wharf, but his parents cannot. "Falling through the cracks" is a common phrase for something that has slipped one's attention or control, something that may be sad but can't be fixed or undone—something like an adolescent's diminished connection to his or her parents. Falling is one of the most common and terrifying experiences in dreaming, but it usually involves the dreamer, not another character. In Paul's dream his parents fall out of the scene, abruptly dropping out of his life. This is his path to follow, not theirs.

Later events in Paul's life cast an interesting light on the archetypal conflict at the center of his dream. When he was nineteen he began training as a Catholic priest, and he served the church for thirty years until he left the order, married a former nun, and raised a family of three children. To become a priest is, by design, a dramatic break with ordinary relationships (such as with one's parents) and a total dedication to otherworldly ideals. Seen in this light, his recurrent dreams anticipated the magnitude of the religious transformation ahead of him. Perhaps the dream even anticipated his later transformation after he left the priesthood, when the church could no longer stay with him in the next stage of his life's journey. Formal religion fell out of his life, dropping through the cracks in the wharf, as he followed the new path of fathering a family. His teenage nightmare became a "root metaphor" that encapsulated a fundamental theme running throughout his life.

By this point in the book, we hope that readers have gained a good familiarity with our basic approach to children's big dreams. Now we would like to change our method of presentation. Instead of focusing on single dreams, we will discuss clusters of dreams that share a particular theme with archetypal dimensions. We have chosen two clusters of dreams from children at various ages, one a cluster of fire dreams, and a second of what we call "titanic" dreams. These are not the only themes worth studying in children's dreams, but we found several good examples of them in our research and we felt they could help teach readers how to appreciate the multiple possibilities of meaning in dreams with archetypal symbolism.

We have already discussed a few dreams involving fire ("The Bunny I Left Behind," "The Wayfarer's Church," "The Robber's Den"), and with each one we pointed out some of the common meanings associated with this powerful element. Of course, every dream has its own personal context that influences the range of its possible significance. A dream of fire will mean one thing for a child whose house just burned down, and something different for a child sick with a raging fever, and something different again for a child raised with religious teachings about "fire and brimstone." We are not saying all fire dreams have the same meaning. Rather, we are trying to highlight the archetypal themes that frequently recur in many (but not necessarily all) children's dreams involving fire.

## FIRE IN THE DEPARTMENT STORE

### *"Emmy"*

*I am at the Emporium Department Store, a single big building. A huge parking lot is all around it. I am on the second floor staring down huge wide stairs that are carpeted. I have my doll baby in her little stroller.*

*Fire breaks out. People are rushing down the stairs. I start down the stairs, get halfway to a wide landing and stop, not knowing what to do. Then I realize the fire is enclosed in a plexiglass rectangle, floor to ceiling with stairs rising around it.*

*Locale:* The dream takes place inside a department store that's generally familiar but different on the inside.

*Exposition:* She is standing at the top of a wide staircase, with her doll and baby stroller.

*Peripeteia:* There's a fire, and people hurry downstairs to escape. She starts hurrying downstairs, too.

*Lysis:* She sees the fire is contained inside a plexiglass structure.

(Emmy was six to seven years old when she had this dream.)


## THE HOUSE MIGHT COLLAPSE

### *"Steve"*

*My dream started at the bottom of the stairs at home. The entire house was on fire, a huge blaze. The hallway filled with smoke black as a cloudy midnight sky. From the base up the stairwell to the first landing the walls and stairs were replaced by fast burning fire. I was terrified that the house might collapse. Then I remembered the glass door upstairs leading to the outside, and ran for it. I felt enormous concern for my family's safety. I thought I was moving fast but was only moving at a casual pace. I made the u-turn halfway up the stairs and realized that from there up there was no fire at all. I ran up and out the glass door. Instead of running off the roof onto the hillside I went the opposite way to the edge of the roof in front of the house and carefully jumped off. However, before I could turn around the dream always ended and I would wake up.*

*Locale:* The setting is his family home. He worries about his family, but they never actually appear.

*Exposition:* He's at the bottom of the stairs, and his house is on fire.

*Peripeteia:* He goes up the stairs, through the glass door, and out of the house.

*Lysis:* The dream ends with him jumping from the roof.

(This was a recurrent dream that came when Steve was seven to eight years old.)

## AT HOME ON THE REZ

### "Penny"

*I just had this dream not too long ago. I was at home on the rez and my whole family was there and all my cousins were there. I felt really happy because we were all together; we made a fire and cooked outside. And then everything changed in the dream. We weren't on the rez, we were at Disneyland. I loved this dream. I was happy in the dream to go to Disneyland with my cousins.*

*Locale:* She is at home on the reservation where her Native American family lives. Later the reservation changes to Disneyland. A large number of family relatives are present.

*Exposition:* She is together with her family and cousins.

*Peripeteia:* They make a fire and cook; then they have shifted to Disneyland where they continue their pleasant time together.

*Lysis:* She awakens happy.

(Penny is a fourteen-year-old Native American girl.)

## ENCIRCLED BY FIRE DINOSAURS

### "Larry"

*In the dream I awoke in my bedroom to find it ablaze, flames leaping up the walls, no great heat or smoke. I was terrified and desperate* to escape. *The bedroom door was covered in flame so I climbed out the window over my bed that led onto a porch roof. Unexpectedly I was on an endless blue plain. I turned around to go back to the house but now the entire place was ablaze, flame pouring from the windows and it was not my house. I started running across the parallel lines of the plain of that infinite flat surface. Now I was being pursued by the fire itself in the form of fiery dinosaurs. I was afraid of being burned, not eaten. They caught up with me, completely encircling me in bright orange flame.*

*Locale:* The setting starts in his bedroom, but then shifts to a fantastic place outside his home, a vast blue plain. No other characters are present.

*Exposition:* He wakes up and finds his bedroom on fire.

*Peripeteia:* He climbs out a window to escape and is surprised to be in a very strange realm where the fire now follows him in the form of monstrous prehistoric creatures.

*Lysis:* He is surrounded by the fire, with no way to escape.

(This was a recurrent dream that came to science fiction and horror writer Lawrence Watt-Evans, born in 1954, when he was seven to nine years old.)

We could describe more examples, but these should be enough to give you a sense of the many different ways in which a single element can appear in children's dreams. Each of these four dreams puts fire at the center of the story. In three of the dreams, fire appears as a threatening force of destruction. In Emmy's dream the department store has caught fire and people are rushing out in a panic. In Steve's and Larry's dreams they are trying to escape the flames that threaten to consume their homes. These dreams initially portray fire as a wild, uncontrollable danger that must be escaped.

But then the dreams shift to a different view of fire. Emmy stops running down the stairs and sees the fire has somehow been contained within a tall structure made of plexiglass. Steve discovers the fire is not burning the top half of the staircase. There's no heat or smoke from the fire in Larry's house, and when he flees outside he lands in an entirely different kind of reality. In each case the dreamer finds something new and unexpected, something to wonder about. The fire changes the dreamer's perspective, showing them something they had never seen before.

Penny's dream recalls our earlier discussion of "The Robber's Den" and "The Wayfarer's Church," two dreams in which fire appeared as a symbol of hearth and home. As a young Native American girl, the "rez" or reservation is the home of Penny's family and culture, a sanctuary from the encroachment of white culture. Gathering around a fire and cooking food with one's family is a deep pleasure not just for Native Americans but for virtually all humans throughout our evolutionary history. A hearth fire is a primal setting of comfort, warmth, security, and nurturance, and children naturally feel drawn toward it, in waking and dreaming.

Like the other three dreams, Penny's has a surprising shift of perspective following the appearance of fire. In her case, she and her cousins suddenly go to Disneyland. This shift might seem like an unfortunate move from the sublime to the ridiculous, from indigenous cultural authenticity to American consumerist fantasy. But Penny did not describe it that way. In her experience of the dream, the shift to Disneyland had the effect of extending and amplifying the happy family feelings of the first part of the dream, carrying it into a new setting. Penny's emerging identity loves the comfort of the reservation *and* the excitement of Disneyland. That suggests her developmental challenge will be to integrate those two dramatically different cultural influences within her emerging adult personality.

The other dreams also portray challenges for future integration. Emmy's dream starts with a playful anticipation of her future identity as a mother (the doll and baby carriage), then threatens her with fire, mass panic, and the temptation to follow the crowd hurtling downstairs. But her fear is relieved by the sudden appearance of the plexiglass structure, which contains the fire and holds it safely. The fire becomes a feature of the department store, aligned with its architecture like an artistic enhancement of the space. This strange but reassuring image suggests that the fire's energy can be managed and channeled in useful ways. It can be integrated into the overall design of Emmy's physical and psychological world.

Steve's recurrent fire dream ends with him jumping from his burning home but not yet reorienting himself on the ground. As with Brenda's dream in chapter 3 ("The Bunny I Left Behind"), escaping up and out of a burning home appears in Steve's dream as a metaphor of growing up. The suspended lysis reflects the uncertainty about where this process is leading him. He has found the right way to escape and he feels anxious about his family, but he does not yet know where he is going. That's his future developmental challenge: shifting his awareness from what his life has been to what it's becoming.

Larry's dream, as befits a future writer of science fiction and fantasy literature, leads from fire into more speculative realms of the imagination. His dream is actually a hybrid of a fire dream and the "titanic" theme we will discuss in the next cluster of dreams.

In previous research Kelly has described a rare type of dream he refers to as "titanic" because such dreams seem to transport people to a dizzying realm of cosmic forces and elemental realities. In ancient Greek mythology the Titans were the generation of gods *before* the Olympian gods Zeus, Hera, and the others. The Titans came from a time before life on earth began, before any normal features of human reality had taken shape. The Titans have no personality, no mind or consciousness as we know it. They represent cosmic forces whose epic battles have shaped the reality in which we live.

Titanic dreams happen very infrequently, but when they occur they make an extremely vivid and long-lasting impact on the dreamer's memory. They are more common in childhood than later in life, and we wanted to make sure readers have some background should they ever encounter this uncanny, vertiginous type of dream.

## GRAY STONES

### "Felix"

*There is a room with three large gray stones rotating all together. They roll on and on, then start to waver and it appears they will topple or fly off. I wake in a cold sweat, scared as I could be.*

*Locale:* The setting is a nondescript room, with no characters. The dreamer seems to be observing rather than participating in the dream.

*Exposition:* The gray stones are rotating and rolling.

*Peripeteia:* The stones move even more energetically, threatening to burst apart in a fast, unpredictable, dangerous fashion.

*Lysis:* He awakens in fear.

(This was a recurrent dream for Felix between the ages of six and twelve.)

## THE STARS ABOVE

### "Trudy"

*I can only remember a huge dark sky filled with lots of stars. This dream recurred many times and what I remember most was the feeling it left me with every time. I felt very small and insignificant in relation to the sky and stars.*

*Locale:* She is outside by herself.

*Exposition:* She looks up at the night sky.

*Peripeteia:* No action occurs. She just looks up.

*Lysis:* She awakens with a feeling of deep humility and existential finitude.

(Trudy was about eight years old when she had this recurrent dream.)

## NUCLEAR WAR

### "Ronnie"

*In the dream, there's a nuclear war going on. I'm in the middle of a desolate field. It is very dark out. There are lots of dead trees spread out. They are all knotted and gnarly looking but they are still standing. There is a very large Russian bomber jet flying overhead. Bombs with parachutes attached to them start slowly falling from the plane. None of them hit the ground. I'm standing there realizing this is the end of the universe. No one else is around. Everyone else is dead . . . and there I stand.*

*Locale:* He's in a desolate field by himself.

*Exposition:* A nuclear war has broken out.

*Peripeteia:* He notices the dead trees. An enemy plane drops bombs.

*Lysis:* The dream ends with an apocalyptic realization of the end of the universe.

(This was a recurrent dream that started when Ronnie was five years old.)

## THE SECRET OF THE UNIVERSE

### "John"

*I pick up a large object far too big for me to physically lift and it is two things at once: it is vast and heavy and it is tiny and weightless. It is very distinctly both things yet both occupying the same space. It feels as though I hold the secret of the universe and it is the dream I believe in.*

*Locale:* The setting is unspecified. There are no other characters.

*Exposition:* He picks up a very large object.

*Peripeteia:* He realizes the object is both heavy and weightless.

*Lysis:* He awakens with a sense of knowing a great truth.

(This was a recurrent childhood dream of fantasy writer John Gordon, born 1925.)

Titanic dreams usually have no characters or any other form of organic life besides the dreamer. The settings often have a dizzying sense of infinite magnitude, disembodied abstraction, and precise geometric structure. Whatever happens in the dream is driven by elemental forces of gravity, mass, speed, and entropy. The dreamer, having no power to resist or defend against these forces, merely witnesses their actions and effects. Such dreams are difficult to put into words, and they rarely elicit any associations or memories from current daily life. They seem to pull back the veil of our world's appearance to show what's really happening here and throughout the universe. Wherever titanic dreams come from, they provoke in the dreamer a quantum leap in awareness of the ultimate physical powers shaping the cosmos.

In many titanic dreams this radically transcendent perspective leads to distressing feelings of confusion, vulnerability, and inescapable danger. Felix's dream of the madly spinning stones does not sound especially scary, but he experienced it as utterly terrifying. Ronnie's dream envisions an apocalyptic war that destroys all life by the use of nuclear bombs, weapons that release the deadly power of atomic forces. We don't know where he learned, as a five-year-old, about nuclear bombs, but it seems likely he recognized this was the worst fear of the adults in his culture, and thus it could serve as an effective dream metaphor of his own darkest apprehensions. In each of these dreams the child reacts to the discovery of titanic realities with personal fear and existential dread.

With greater knowledge of the universe comes a greater sense of the frailty of human life within it.

Trudy's awe-inspiring vision of the stars above represents the rare phenomenon of a positive titanic dream. She too witnesses a reality beyond this earthly existence, and she too realizes how small and insignificant she is in that new cosmic perspective. But for her the experience does not threaten her with immediate annihilation. She is able to maintain her emotional composure as she contemplates the starry vault of heaven and begins the process of reorienting herself within the universe. Her dream could be amplified in connection with the Book of Job and God's concluding speech out of the whirlwind, which humbles the ego but opens the whole self to a wider awareness of the wonders of creation.

John's dream of the strangely light-yet-heavy object confronts him with a paradox that tests the limits of his understanding. His mind struggles to grasp the possibility of an object that is massively heavy and weightless at the same time. The binary categories that govern his ordinary life make this seem impossible, but at some level John intuitively realizes that it's *true*, polar opposites *can* be integrated into a single entity. Perhaps he had learned in school that weight is relative to gravity, so an object may seem heavy in a place with strong gravity and light in a place with weak gravity. Perhaps he didn't know anything about such matters before his dream gave him an experiential lesson in this fundamental fact of physics. Either way, it impressed him as a truth of profound importance that continues to inspire him more than half a century later:

> It is likely that I write only because I dream. The doors we dare not go through when we are awake are open to us when we dream, and writing fiction is one way of getting back through those doors. . . . The usefulness of our dreams is that they subvert our waking state, but it can only be wakefulness that makes them into something more than mere dreams.

The dreams of late childhood and early adolescence reflect the tremendous changes in body, mind, social identity, and existential awareness that occur at this time of life. These dreams harken back to earlier stages of life, just as the dreams from early childhood look ahead to adolescence and beyond. This is why, by the end of this chapter, we set aside the age divisions and opened up the discussion to consider recurrent themes that can be found in dreams across all ages of childhood, and indeed throughout the life cycle. We want readers to be comfortable exploring the meanings of dreams in both of these directions: in developmental terms, as a reflection of a child's age and maturity, and in archetypal terms, as an instance of recurrent symbolic themes found in the dreams of people at all ages.

# 6

# NURTURING THE IMAGINATION
# IN CHILDHOOD AND BEYOND

In this final chapter we step back and take a more practical look at how to cultivate dreaming and the imagination in childhood. If you ask anyone involved in childcare and education, they will likely agree on the vital importance of helping children develop healthy and creative imaginations. Yet children today rarely get any information about dreams or support in trying to understand their dreaming experiences. Dreaming is one of the earliest activities of each child's imagination, and it can become a lifelong resource of creative insight and archetypal wisdom—but our society does almost nothing to teach children about these powers that naturally emerge within their nightly slumber. This is a cultural disconnect we hope our book will help to remedy.

For parents, teachers, and counselors who believe in the importance of nurturing children's imaginations, we have written this chapter to give you several dream-based ideas for boosting the creative powers of children at any age, in virtually any circumstance. Dreams have many advantages as a resource for parenting, education, and therapy. For one thing, they cost nothing—they're free! They occur effortlessly, available to all children and all people throughout their lives. Dreams speak in a language of direct personal relevance to the dreamer, so there's no need for an expert's advice (though it may be helpful to get someone else's perspective—more on that below). Most children are naturally curious about dreams and interested in talking about them, so it really takes very little effort to open up the subject and provide them with useful information and support.

## SLEEP PATTERNS

To boost children's dream awareness, a good place to start is with the patterns of their sleep. A healthy dream life depends on a healthy sleep life, something that many children in contemporary society do not enjoy. According to the National Sleep Foundation, children in the three- to five-year age range need 11–13 hours of sleep per day (nighttime plus naps), and children five to twelve need 10–11 hours of sleep each night. Many children get much less sleep than this, however. Over time a sleep deficit can harm children in many aspects of their lives: diminishing their physical vitality, weakening their immune systems, making them less alert in school, less capable of processing new information, less able to control their impulses and emotions. Of course, parents and teachers may not notice these problems because they are sleep deprived themselves! It's really a society-wide issue that has not received as much public attention as it should.

A good way to start promoting healthier sleep habits is to evaluate the setting of where sleep happens. For parents, we recommend you take a look at your children's bedrooms and assess them in terms of how well they support a good night's sleep. Is there anything you can do to make the room feel safer and more comfortable, to protect it from light and noise, to keep the air at a fresh and even temperature? We also suggest reviewing your children's typical activities in the hour before bedtime. What can you do to encourage a smooth transition from waking to sleeping? Sugary foods and drinks do not help the bedtime process, and neither do computers, video games, loud music, or television. What are the presleep rituals your children enjoy the most? It could be reading or telling stories, drinking a glass of milk, praying, or properly arranging their stuffed animals. Whatever activities your children find most relaxing as they get into bed, you can help them maintain those presleep habits. You might also examine the conditions in which your children wake up in the morning. Do your children have time to wake up gradually, or are they compelled to spring out of bed immediately and jump into the daily schedule? Do they ever get to sleep in, as long as they naturally want to?

We are not advocating impossibly high standards of parenting or criticizing anyone who falls short—we've raised children ourselves and we know that unforeseen issues and challenges come every day and every night. We simply want to support you in identifying aspects of your children's activities and environment that impact their sleep, both positively and negatively. Some of these factors are easy to change, others not so much. We believe no matter what you try, you can be confident that *any* improvements you make in the quality of your children's sleep will promote their physical and emotional welfare, strengthen the workings of their imagination, and make it easier to dream.

## DREAM JOURNALING

As we noted in the introduction, a distinctive quality of big dreams is that they are literally unforgettable, indelibly burned into a person's memory for a lifetime. But most dreams are more fragile than that. If you don't write them down upon awakening they are quickly lost. In our view that is not necessarily a tragedy; if you forget a dream with an important message from the collective unconscious, you can be sure another dream will come to seek your attention. We trust in the natural ebb and flow of dream recall. Whatever you remember is worth paying attention to; whatever you forget will, if needed, find its way back to you in a future dream.

Keeping a dream journal is the ideal way of preserving your dream memories and following more closely the unfolding development of your imagination. A "journal" can be as simple as a pad of paper or as elaborate as a decorated, multisection notebook. The key is that it has to be safe, private, and easily accessible so new dreams can be written down soon after awakening. As a parent, teacher, or counselor, you can encourage children to keep dream journals as a fun and enlightening source of self-knowledge. Some children are natural writers who keep a diary from an early age. For them, all that's needed is the suggestion to include their dreams as possible writing topics in their diaries. For other children, the adults can start as dream journal stenographers, writing down what the children tell them and keeping the reports in a safe place.

It doesn't matter how often children add new dreams to the journal; more is not necessarily better. What's important is having a consistent, readily available place for recording any significant dreams that might occur. A dream journal is like an open invitation to the imagination, welcoming any and all comers. It lets the child's unconscious know that its expressions will be heard, remembered, and integrated into waking awareness. In this sense a journal does not simply preserve dreams from the past, it also opens the mind to new dreams in the future.

Over time a dream journal can become a precious personal document that chronicles the psychological and spiritual course of a child's life. It enables children to see meaningful patterns in their experiences and recognize the complicated emotional depths of their relationships with family and friends. More than anything, it holds up a mirror that shows children the strange and wonderfully creative powers of their own imaginations.

## DREAMING AND ART

More than thirty thousand years ago, communities of Paleolithic humans in the southern Mediterranean created a network of cave paintings that have been described by modern archeologists as a "creative explosion." A recent film by Werner Herzog, *Cave of Forgotten Dreams*, provides a rare glimpse of one of the most spectacular of these caves in Lascaux, France. No one knows for sure why the people painted these amazing, fantastic images, but it seems increasingly clear that the paintings were designed in such a way as to produce a strong psychological impact on their viewers. When people went down into the caves, with torches casting ever-changing shadows on the walls and their footsteps echoing strangely in the subterranean acoustics, they could not help but enter into a dreamlike state of awareness. Perhaps some of the paintings deep within the caves were based on dreams. Many of the images (animals, distorted humans, geometric shapes) do correspond to prominent features of big dream content. Perhaps people even slept in the caves and practiced dream incubation, that is, rituals to evoke a divine dream, as shamans have been known to do in various cultures around the world. Many questions remain about these ancient cave artists, but everything we know points to their recognition of a fundamental kinship between dreaming, art, and the imagination.

We believe this historical context supports the practice of exploring dreams through playful artistic expression. Most children are enthusiastic and highly creative artists, especially when they are young and unaware of what art "should" look like. It takes no great effort to weave dreams into their artistic activities. All a parent or teacher has to do is make the suggestion and let the child's imagination take it from there. Some possibilities include:

- Drawing or painting a picture of a dream, perhaps focusing on a particular image or scene, or making a map of where the dream took place.
- Reenacting the dream with dolls, action figures, or sand tray toys.
- Making something out of clay, wood, Lego, or another material to represent a character or object from a dream.

- Writing a story or a poem about a dream.
- Making a song to express in music the dream's images, feelings, and actions.
- Playacting a dream, pretending to be the characters.

In all these media, the child may want to go beyond the dream to explore different endings, try alternative strategies of behavior, amplify a feeling, or add characters or themes from other stories. That's okay, of course—the whole point of art is the freedom to create. Dreams are like springboards of innovation that stimulate the artistic process. Where the process leads is less important than getting it going in the first place.

All of these art activities can be done individually or in groups, in a class setting or at home. If a child feels comfortable creating something artistic based on a scary dream or nightmare, it can be a cathartic experience that enables the child to treat the dream as raw material for a self-chosen project. The child is no longer a passive recipient of nightmare emotions but an active creator who can integrate the bad dreams into something new and artistically interesting.

Another approach to nurturing the imagination in children is by telling stories about dreaming. Two of the all-time classics of children's literature center on dreams: *Alice's Adventures in Wonderland* by Lewis Carroll and *Where the Wild Things Are* by Maurice Sendak. The delight so many generations of children have taken in these stories comes from their inspiring portrayal of the magical creativity of dreaming. The fictional adventures of Alice and Max resonate with the real-life dream experiences of children at all ages, giving them a glimpse of the creative potentials in their own imaginations. Appendix 2 at the end of the book gives other suggestions of children's stories relating to dreams.

The same can be said of the Harry Potter novels by J. K. Rowling, which are filled with dreams that express deep emotional truths and symbolic anticipations of Harry's adventures through the series. These hugely popular novels portray dreaming very sympathetically as a genuine bit of magic that is also accessible to "Muggles" (nonmagical folk). Appendix 3 describes and analyzes all the dreams in the seven Harry Potter novels. We hope this will be a resource for parents and teachers who read these stories with their children and want to point out how Harry's fictional dreams give insight into the actual dreaming potentials of real children.

## SHARING DREAMS WITH OTHER PEOPLE

As long as humans have been dreaming, they have been talking about their dreams with other people. Anthropologists have found that virtually all indigenous cultures have traditions of dream-sharing as a normal part of community life. People in modern Western society often have less experience with dream-sharing, but once they give it a try, it's like fish taking to water. We are all dreamers, and we all intuitively resonate with the dreaming experiences of other people.

To share a dream is to share a personal expression of the psyche, so it requires a sense of trust, safety, and respect among everyone involved. Dream-sharing enables people to communicate at a level of deep emotional honesty. To learn the most from the process, everyone must feel comfortable and confident that whatever they say will be treated with respect.

A good way of establishing that kind of respect is to be aware of your own projections. If someone else (a child or adult) tells you a dream, your reactions and responses will stem from *your* version of that dream. Only the dreamer has direct access to the original dream; you do not, and so any comments you make are limited by that fact. To stay conscious of this, we like to use the prefacing phrase of Jeremy Taylor and Montague Ullman, "*If it were my dream* . . ." Instead of telling someone, "Your dream means *x*," we would say, "If that were my dream, it would mean *x*." This may seem a subtle distinction, but we believe it's important because the only real trouble you can get into with sharing dreams is imposing your projections onto the dreamer. Even if you really, really, *really* think you know what another person's dream means, you can never know for sure because it's not your dream. However, if you preface your comments with "If it were my dream . . . ," you can express the same ideas in a form that gives the other person a chance to ponder whether or not they apply to the dream.

In many cases it may not be practical to go through Jung's four-part dramatic structure when a person shares a dream with you, but you might want to use it in your own mind as you listen. Where is the dream set, and who's in it (locale)? What's happening at the start of the dream (exposition)? What happens next (peripeteia)? How does it end (lysis)? These four categories can give you a quick orientation to the dream and highlight special areas for possible exploration.

Rather than diving right into a comprehensive interpretation, we suggest you start by asking questions about the details of the dream, to build up as clear an image of it in your mind as possible. Some aspects of dreams are exquisitely detailed, while others are oddly vague. Don't be surprised if you ask questions the dreamer can't answer, and take note of those elements with the most detail—those may be places where the dreaming imagination has focused special energy.

Once you open the dream up in this way, the discussion can go in several different directions, for as long as everyone feels comfortable and engaged in the process. If the dream includes strong emotions, you could consider the question of where those emotions might appear in waking life. If the dream includes familiar people or places, you could look at how the dream might mirror (or invert) those relationships. If it draws on characters from television, movies, books, and so on, you could explore the metaphorical dimensions of those cultural references. Of course you can amplify the dream and explore its archetypal symbolism, as this book has shown you how to do. What path you follow depends on the type of dream that's shared, the interests of the dreamer, and the time you have to let the conversation unfold.

## FOR TEACHERS

Schoolteachers may feel that dreams are too personal and unpredictable to bring into the classroom. That may seem like a responsible attitude to take, but it neglects the fact that children are constantly dreaming and wondering about their dreams. We encourage teachers at all levels to reconsider the educational opportunities provided by children's natural curiosity about dreaming. If you heard of a new educational resource that was free, available to all children, and inherently interesting to them, wouldn't you want to learn more about it? If this new resource turned out to enhance creativity, empathy, and cognitive maturity, wouldn't it be worth trying to find ways of tapping into its benefits?

The easiest route to dream education with children is through art classes. For all the reasons mentioned above, dreaming can be a powerful source of inspiration for almost any kind of artistic activity. The unpredictability of dreaming becomes an asset in art class, and the personal dimensions can be expressed in ways the child controls and directs.

Literature and writing classes also offer a perfect venue for dream education. When children are doing creative writing projects, the teacher can ask them to write a dream scene for one of their characters. Or they can ask the children to choose one of their own dreams and write a short story or poem about it—this is a good way of addressing the "What do I write about?" question many children ask at the beginning of such projects. When children in a literature class read a book that has a dream scene, the teacher can take the opportunity to discuss the scene carefully, evaluating the role of the dream in the story and connecting it to interesting patterns in current dream research. In science and health education classes, dream education can be supported by including the topic of sleep in the curriculum. The more students know about sleep, the better prepared they will be to understand the nature of dreaming.

Religious educators who teach children in parochial schools or places of worship have many resources to draw upon. In the Abrahamic traditions of Judaism, Christianity, and Islam, the Book of Genesis includes several dream stories that illustrate important ideas about dreaming. Jacob's dream of the heavenly ladder in Genesis 28 carries a powerful message of divine reassurance at a time of personal crisis. Joseph is presented in Genesis 38–40 as a prophetic childhood dreamer and a skilled interpreter who helps the Egyptian pharaoh understand two strange dreams that anticipate future threats to his kingdom. Similarly, in the Book of Daniel the dreams of the Babylonian king Nebuchadnezzar are interpreted by Daniel as prophetic messages that help people change their behavior to prevent possible dangers (Daniel 2:4). In the Christian New Testament, the first two chapters of the Book of Matthew describe five brief dreams that played a helpful role in the story of Jesus's birth. The Qur'an of Islam includes the story of Joseph's interpretation of Pharaoh's dreams, and in the hadiths (sayings of the Prophet) Muhammad asks his followers to share their dreams with him each morning, especially dreams that might have spiritual meaning and community significance.

The same could be said of Buddhism, Hinduism, and other religious traditions, all of which have sacred stories presenting dreams as one of the ways humans connect with the divine, however the divine may be conceptualized. For religious educators, dreams offer a personally engaging means of teaching students about the core teachings of your faith. Dreams also offer a subject that can help students see deep connections across many different faiths, so they can better appreciate and respect the religious beliefs and practices of other people.

## FOR THERAPISTS

Our approach in this book has assumed the children are not suffering from any particular emotional problems or psychopathology when we interpret their dreams. If, however, a child is having trouble distinguishing reality from fantasy, or is deeply depressed, or has been a victim of abuse or trauma, we recommend the child's caregivers seek the advice of a physician. The dreams and nightmares of troubled children are usually related to their psychological problems, so it's worth paying close attention to them. The dreams may also have archetypal dimensions like those discussed in this book, but expressed in images relevant to the child's particular set of problems. We do not present our approach as a form of therapy, although it did originate in Jung's practice as a clinical psychiatrist and can easily be applied in therapeutic contexts.

Today very few therapists receive any training or instruction in working with dreams, archetypally or otherwise. The rise of cognitive-behavioral approaches as the favored mode of therapy has pushed dream interpretation to the margins of clinical practice. Cognitive-behavioral therapy emphasizes short-term efforts to change patterns of waking thought. Working with dreams, by contrast, can take a long time and lead into realms of the psyche far removed from waking thought (though ultimately returning with an enriched perspective on present-day life). The fruits of interpreting a dream include a deeper sense of self-knowledge, a wider range of questions to ask about human existence, and a heightened sensitivity to creative potentials in the waking world. In today's mental health care system, these kinds of outcomes are often seen as too vague and unmeasurable to merit clinical use or insurance reimbursement.

However, a recognition of the therapeutic value of dream interpretation may be on the rise, thanks to research done by Clara Hill and her colleagues at the University of Maryland. Hill has developed and extensively tested a psychotherapeutic method of working with dreams that is simple to learn and provides therapeutically useful insights to both the client and therapist in a relatively short time. Anyone who practices cognitive-behavioral therapy can easily integrate Hill's method into his or her work, with the confidence that this approach is grounded in well-established principles of effective psychotherapy, with a great deal of empirical data to support it. The participants in Hill's research reported gaining more depth, insight, and satisfaction with their therapy sessions when dream interpretation was included. Our appeal to professional therapists is the same as the one we just made to educators: Many of your clients are innately interested in learning about their dreams, and they will become more engaged in and enthusiastic about the therapeutic process if you create a safe, respectful space for them to explore the creative expressions of their dreaming imaginations.

We especially appreciate the openness of Hill and her colleagues to aspects of dream meaning that touch on religion and spirituality. They recognize that psychotherapy clients often wonder about the spiritual aspects of their dreams, and therapists can learn a great deal if they take these questions seriously and seek connections with the client's waking life situation. We see the archetypal approach presented in this book as compatible with Hill's method, particularly in cases where a client brings an especially vivid, memorable, and/or bizarre dream to the therapist.

## FINAL WORDS

We began this book with a caution to refrain from saying, "*It was just a dream,*" when a child reports a strange or frightening experience of dreaming. Everything we have written in the book is intended to provide you with alternative responses for that situation, responses that affirm rather than dismiss the creative power of children's dreams. For example, you could say "*Yes, it was a dream! You are a dreamer, and so am I. We are all dreamers!*" This is in fact a true statement, and once children realize that dreaming is an innate experience of the human imagination, their fear of the unknown diminishes and their natural curiosity and enthusiasm about dreaming can blossom.

We cannot predict what exactly you or your children will discover in dreams. We do, however, agree with Jung's emphasis on the tremendous value of these dreaming insights when he spoke of big dreams in childhood as "the richest jewel in the treasure house of the soul." Whatever language or metaphors you prefer to use, we feel confident your own experiences will teach you about the deep and valuable impact of these dreams and their lasting influence on a child's psychological and spiritual development through life.

# Appendix 1

## A LIST OF THE DREAMS DISCUSSED IN THIS BOOK

### CHAPTER 3: DREAMS OF EARLY CHILDHOOD

### CHAPTER 4: DREAMS OF MIDDLE CHILDHOOD

## CHAPTER 5: DREAMS OF
## LATE CHILDHOOD AND ADOLESCENCE

# Appendix 2

## CHILDREN'S STORIES RELATING TO DREAMS

Here is a list of our favorite stories about dreams for children. We have grouped them in order of age relevance. The first few titles are best for very young children, and the last ones more appropriate for older children.

*Where the Wild Things Are*, written and illustrated by Maurice Sendak (Harper and Row, 1963). The award-winning story of a rebellious boy named Max who falls asleep and dreams of sailing to a mysterious island, where he becomes King of the Wild Things. Sendak beautifully expresses the unruly inner impulses that children struggle to control in both their waking and dreaming lives.

*The Nutcracker Ballet*: A classic that has also been rendered in countless children's books, the story tells of the dream adventures experienced one Christmas Eve by a young girl named Clara, with fascinating connections between waking events and dreaming visions. A tale that vividly evokes the special magic of Christmas dreams.

*Caps for Sale: A Tale of a Peddler, Some Monkeys and Their Monkey Business*, written and illustrated by Esphyr Slobodkina (Live Oak Media, 2004). A peddler of caps sits down under a tree for a nap, and is surprised by a troop of mischievous monkeys. The sudden appearance and disappearance of the monkeys makes you wonder if the whole experience was a dream.

*There's a Nightmare in My Closet*, written and illustrated by Mercer Mayer (Dial Books, 1968). A boy is scared of a horrible monster who lives in his closet, and he tries to fight him off—until the boy realizes the monster is scared of *him*. A touching fable that illustrates Jung's idea about embracing the shadow.

*When Cats Dream*, written and illustrated by Dav Pilkey (Orchard Books, 1992). This delightful story begins with the quiet, un-eventful life of cats during the day, and *then* plunges into the wild, colorful world of cats dreaming (with nods to Picasso and other modern artists).

*Just a Dream*, written and illustrated by Chris Van Allsburg (Houghton Mifflin, 1990). A boy thoughtlessly throws away some garbage, then goes to sleep that night and dreams of a future world smothered in pollution and smog. This cautionary envi-ronmental fable draws on the real power of dreams to imagine what will come in the future if we humans do not change our consciousness of nature.

*The Boy Who Dreamed of an Acorn*, written by Leigh Casler, il-lustrated by Shonto Begay (Philomel Books, 1994). This book is based on the rite of the vision quest, practiced by many Native American cultures as a way of initiating children into their spiritual traditions. A wonderful story that suggests dreaming is a source of lifelong guidance and personal destiny.

*Alice's Adventures in Wonderland*, written by Lewis Carroll (vari-ous editions). This is the best-known dream adventure in all of children's literature. Younger children will certainly delight in the comic mishaps of Alice's tour through Wonderland, but the story is really aimed at older children who are able to appreciate the playful, subversive paradoxes that emerge in Alice's long, strange dream.

*The Dream Pillow*, written and illustrated by Mitra Modarressi (Orchard Books, 1994). This book draws on the American folk practice of making dream pillows with special herbs and flowers to inspire good dreams. It gives children a sense that sharing and understanding dreams can be an important means to true friendship.

*The Great Kapok Tree*, written and illustrated by Lynne Cherry (Gulliver Books, 1990). A man goes into the Amazon rain forest to chop down a huge kapok tree. He tires, and takes a nap, and as he sleeps the creatures of the jungle who depend on this tree for their lives come to the man and whisper in his ear, asking him not to chop it down. The story highlights the power of dreaming to reveal our deep relationship with the natural world.

*The Wizard of Oz* (1939, directed by Victor Fleming). Although originating as a series of books by L. Frank Baum, the movie version has perhaps the most magical rendering of a child's dream experience ever created. Very young children may be too frightened by the Wicked Witch of the West and her flying monkeys, but children at all other ages will resonate with this timeless tale of a fantastic dream journey that weaves daily experiences with deep unconscious truths.

# Appendix 3

# THE DREAMS AND NIGHTMARES OF HARRY POTTER

This appendix first appeared as an article in *Dream Time* magazine (Spring 2011, vol. 8, no. 2, pp. 14–17, 37–38). We have included it here to give readers another source of insight into the recurrent themes and archetypal patterns of children's dreams.

More than four hundred million people, most of them children and teenagers, have read the Harry Potter novels of J. K. Rowling, immersing themselves in a fantastical world in which broomsticks fly, portraits talk, wizards cast spells—and dreams reveal honest emotional truths. Rowling's hugely popular stories about the magical education of young Harry Potter abound with dream experiences that weave prophetic visions with psychologically astute insights into adolescent feelings of loss, fear, desire, and hope. Looking closely at the roles played by dreaming across all seven novels, it becomes clear that readers of these books are well primed to regard dreams as a piece of magic, as a mysterious, potentially dangerous, but extremely valuable source of power, meaning, and guidance in life. Rowling's fantasy tale carries a message of real-world significance: We Muggles (nonwizards) may not be able to fly on brooms or cast spells, but we do possess the magical power of dreaming.

The first time we meet Harry, in the opening pages of *Harry Potter and the Sorcerer's Stone*, he is waking up in the tiny coat closet where his dim-witted Muggle relatives the Dursleys have kept him hidden for the past ten years. Harry "rolled onto his back and tried to remember the dream he had been having. It had been a good one. There had been a flying motorcycle in it. He had a funny feeling he'd had the same dream before." When Harry mentions the dream to the Dursleys on a family drive to the zoo, Mr. Dursley, introduced to readers as someone who "didn't approve of imagination," angrily shouts that motorcycles don't fly. Taken aback, Harry replies, "I know they don't, it was only a dream." What he does not yet know is that motorcycles *do* fly when properly enchanted, and a flying motorcycle in fact brought him to the Dursleys' house ten years ago. His recurrent dream is not "only" a dream, but rather a meaningful and reassuring reminder of his true origins, despite the best efforts of the stubbornly pedestrian Dursleys to erase those memories from his mind. This early debate about the significance of dreams establishes a basic tension running through all the novels between the infinite potentials of the wizarding world and the anxious Muggle determination to pretend that such potentials do not exist.

After the disastrous zoo visit, when Harry discovers he can speak to snakes and sets one loose on his cousin Dudley, the flying motorcycle returns to spirit him away on a journey to Hogwarts School of Witchcraft and Wizardry, Harry's home for the next several years. On his first night at Hogwarts,

> Perhaps Harry had eaten a bit too much, because he had a very strange dream. He was wearing Professor Quirrell's turban, which kept talking to him, telling him he had to transfer to Slytherin at once, because it was his destiny. Harry told the turban he did not want to be in Slytherin; it got heavier and heavier; he tried to pull it off but it tightened painfully—and there was Malfoy, laughing at him as he struggled with it—then Malfoy turned into the hook-nosed teacher, Snape, whose laugh became high and cold—there was a burst of green light and Harry awoke, sweating and shaking. He rolled over and fell asleep again, and when he woke the next day, he didn't remember the dream at all.

It's too bad Harry forgets the dream, because it accurately reveals his ultimate challenge in this book and throughout the series: to defeat this malevolent lineage of characters from Slytherin, one of the four houses at Hogwarts, infamous for its attraction to dark magic. Draco Malfoy, Harry's bitter rival and classmate, is a member of Slytherin house and Professor Snape, Harry's least favorite teacher, is Slytherin house master. Though Harry does not know it yet, the high, cold laugh and the voice talking from Professor Quirrell's turban come from his archenemy, the dark wizard known as Lord Voldemort (himself a former Slytherin student). The burst of green light shows Harry what a killing curse looks like—something he has seen once before, ten years earlier, when Voldemort murdered his parents.

None of this registers consciously for Harry, but it's all laid out for readers in his first-night-at-Hogwarts dream. The talking turban directly foreshadows the climactic discovery at the end of this book that Voldemort (a tiny, shriveled being at this point) is controlling Quirrell by hiding inside the back of his turban. More broadly, the fact that Harry himself is wearing the turban anticipates a series-long struggle with his "inner Voldemort," a struggle in which his lightning-scarred head is the primary battleground.

As the story unfolds Harry learns more about his past, the death of his parents, and his strange connection to Voldemort. Now he begins having recurrent nightmares: "Over and over again he dreamed about his parents disappearing in a flash of green light, while a high voice cackled with laughter." By this point Harry recognizes that this horrible scene is not "only" a dream but an actual event that happened in his past. The recurrent nightmares, like his other dreams, turn out to be legitimate memories of horrors in his past. The term "post-traumatic stress disorder" is never used in the books, but readers with clinical training may find it impossible to ignore that diagnosis. The long-buried memories surfacing in his dreams reveal a primal experience of severe, shocking pain.

The second novel, *Harry Potter and the Chamber of Secrets*, also opens with a highly significant dream that Harry ignores. The story starts with an elf servant named Dobby suddenly appearing in his room at the Dursleys' house and begging him not to go back to Hogwarts. Mr. Dursley, furious at this magical intrusion into his well-ordered home, locks Harry in his room, puts metal bars on his window, and leaves him without any food. As night comes,

> Mind spinning over the same unanswerable questions, Harry fell into an uneasy sleep. He dreamed that he was on show in a zoo, with a card reading UNDERAGE WIZARD attached to his cage. People goggled through the bars at him as he lay, starving and weak, on a bed of straw. He saw Dobby's face in the crowd and shouted out, asking for help, but Dobby called, "Harry is safe there, sir!" and vanished. Then the Dursleys appeared and Dudley rattled the bars of the cage, laughing at him. "Stop it," Harry muttered as the rattling pounded in his sore head. "Leave me alone . . . cut it out . . . I'm trying to sleep."

Harry awakens to the sound of his friend Ron Weasley ripping the bars off his window and helping him escape back to Hogwarts. This incorporation of an external stimulus into the dream is a plausible and familiar dream phenomenon, and so is the dream's continuity with Harry's recent interactions with Dobby and the Dursleys.

But the dream's references also extend to broader themes in the story. The first novel began with a visit to the zoo where Dudley taunted a snake, and here at the beginning of the second novel Harry dreams of being in the same position as that captive creature, once again highlighting the eerie affinity he has with serpents. His rare magical ability as a "parsel-mouth," that is, someone who can speak to snakes, comes to the fore in this book as he seeks to unlock the "Chamber of Secrets," where he must battle a massive Basilisk along with a ghostly version of Voldemort. The all-caps reminder of his status as an underage wizard reflects the developmental challenge facing Harry at this stage of the series. His sense of his own magical power is growing rapidly, yet his teachers say he must wait until he's older before using it, even though at this very moment the forces of evil are rising again—the tension of this moral dilemma puts Harry on edge throughout the series. If he doesn't use his power right now, Voldemort may win; but if Harry succumbs to the dark temptations aroused by his own potency, Voldemort may win, too.

In *Harry Potter and the Prisoner of Azkaban* Harry must contend with a new species of wickedness—the Dementors, guards of the wizard prison Azkaban, ghoulish creatures of death and decay who feed on souls and leave their victims empty shells of despair. The Dementors are like PTSD demons, and they affect Harry especially badly. Professor Lupin explains why: Dementors take away everything good inside you so "you'll be left with nothing but the worst experiences of your life. And the worst that has happened to you, Harry, is enough to make anyone fall off their broom." Dementor attacks intermingle with Harry's continuing bad dreams, and now he can distinguish in his memory a specific sound—his mother's scream as Voldemort kills her. At night "Harry dozed fitfully, sinking into dreams full of clammy, rotted hands and petrified pleading, jerking awake to dwell again on his mother's voice." As Harry uncovers more about his past, his initial reaction of wonder and delight at the magical world yields to an acutely painful awareness of the family he never knew and will never have.

Not that everything in Harry's life is going badly. About midway through the third book he helps Gryffindor house win a big Quidditch match (a wizarding sport), and during the match he fights off a (false) Dementor attack by successfully casting a strong though indistinctly shaped Patronus, an advanced-level charm in which the tip of one's wand shoots a jet of silver-white light that takes the form of a specific animal. That night Harry goes to bed feeling better than he has for long time:

> [He] had a very strange dream. He was walking through a forest, his Firebolt [his Quidditch broomstick] over his shoulder, following something silvery-white. It was winding its way through the trees ahead, and he could only catch glimpses of it between the leaves. Anxious to catch up with it, he sped up, but as he moved faster, so did his quarry. Harry broke into a run, and ahead he heard hooves gathering speed. Now he was running flat out, and ahead he could hear galloping. Then he turned a corner into a clearing and—

Suddenly Harry is awakened by a scream. It's Ron, who says Sirius Black, the notorious outlaw, was just in their dorm room. Everyone says Ron must have been dreaming, but Ron insists it really happened.

This premature ending of the dream, just before an eagerly sought moment of final discovery, resonates with common dreaming experience (and with literary history, for example, Coleridge's incomplete *Kublai Khan*). It also makes for a dramatic turn of events, one that Harry, Ron, and the others completely misinterpret. They assume Sirius Black is a Voldemort ally trying to kill Harry, whereas in truth Sirius is Harry's godfather trying to protect Harry from a different agent of the Dark Lord. Harry's father and Sirius were best friends at Hogwarts, and Sirius turns out to be the mysterious donor of the Firebolt broomstick, which Harry received from an unknown source early in the story. Harry's father also played Quidditch, adding another layer of masculine/paternal meaning to the dream.

One need not be a zealous Freudian to recognize the phallic symbolism of flying broomsticks and silvery-white substances coming out of wands. The abrupt awakening from his dream prevents Harry from reflecting on its possible meaning, but when the story reaches its climax we realize the dream has accurately foretold the final turn of the plot. Harry's Patronus charm, when fully formed, takes the shape of a majestic stag—the same animal his father was magically able to turn into. Just when hordes of Dementors have descended upon him, Harry finally understands that even though his father is dead, his paternal memory remains a powerful force that Harry can use to fight his enemies. In his dream Harry takes on the role of a mythic hunter being lured deeper and deeper into the forest in pursuit of an enchanted deer. Here at the end of the story he completes his heroic dream quest by fusing his power with his father's to create a magical force for saving people, not killing them.

Most of Harry's dreams convey meanings related to the battle with Voldemort, but sometimes they reflect his everyday concerns, even if the deeper conflicts are never far away. The night before the final Quidditch match of the season, against the team from Slytherin, Harry "slept badly" and suffered anxious dreams of bizarre misfortunes. This type of dream is familiar to anyone who has tried to sleep while worrying about a big event the next day:

> First he dreamed that he had overslept, and that Wood was yelling, "Where were you? We had to use Neville instead!" Then he dreamed Malfoy and the rest of the Slytherin team arrived for the match riding dragons. He was flying at break-neck speed, trying to avoid a spurt of flames from Malfoy's steed's mouth, when he realized he had forgotten his Firebolt. He fell through the air and woke with a start. It was a few seconds before Harry remembered that the match hadn't taken place yet, that he was safe in bed, and that the Slytherin team definitely wouldn't be allowed to play on dragons.

Wood is the Gryffindor team captain, and Neville is a hapless Gryffindor housemate. The dream is like a prism of Harry's current anxieties, reflecting his concerns about letting down his house, losing a competition to a hated rival, appearing weak in front of his whole school, losing his magical power, losing his ability to fly, and ultimately losing the battle against Slytherin. Harry awakens abruptly with the sensation of falling, another typical dream experience, and he has a moment of waking/dreaming uncertainty. Once fully awake he takes comfort from the fact that the dream is not literally true, although the danger posed by Slytherin's connection to reptilian phallic aggression remains real and ever present.

The fourth book in the series, *Harry Potter and the Goblet of Fire*, marks a big leap in the length (734 pages), psychological depth, and moral complexity of the story. Harry's surprising, unwanted entry into the Triwizard tournament leads to ridicule and social isolation at school. For most of the book he is a solitary, psychologically tormented figure brooding on feelings of shame, fear, and rage. This is a much darker novel that thrusts Harry out of the simple wonders of childhood into the bitter, complicated concerns of the adult world.

As in the first and second novels, he initially appears in book 4 in the act of awakening:

> Harry lay flat on his back, breathing hard as though he had been running. He had awoken from a vivid dream with his hands pressed over his face. . . . Harry tried to recall what he had been dreaming about before he had awoken. It had seemed so real.

Despite the pain in his scar, after a few moments of thought he pieces together the scene revealed by his dream—a Muggle being murdered by Voldemort's snake Nagini. What Harry does not know, but readers do know from the preceding chapter, is that this dream is an accurate, real-time portrayal of something that actually happened. When Harry gets out of bed and writes a letter to Sirius, he decides "there was no point putting in the dream; he didn't want it to look as though he was too worried."

We know this is exactly the wrong thing to do. Ironically, Harry is replicating Mr. Dursley's bias against a troublesome imagination.

From the start of this novel J. K. Rowling sets us up to root *for* Harry's dreams and *against* the skepticism of his waking mind. We know his dreams are indeed telepathic and clairvoyant, giving him a potentially powerful resource in fighting Voldemort. But Harry hesitates in trusting his dreams or telling them to others, unwilling to give people another reason to ridicule him.

While Harry worries about his dream, he also faces the life-threatening challenges of the Triwizard tournament. The night before the second task, which involves finding a way to breathe underwater, Harry anxiously looks for answers in the library, and eventually falls asleep atop his books:

> The mermaid in the painting in the prefects' bathroom was laughing. Harry was bobbing like a cork in bubbly water next to her rock, while she held his Firebolt over his head.
> "Come and get it!" she giggled maliciously. "Come on, jump!"
> "I can't," Harry panted, snatching at the Firebolt, and struggling not to sink. "Give it to me!"
> But she just poked him painfully in the side with the end of the broomstick, laughing at him.

Harry awakens in the library to the anxious poking of Dobby, who tells him what he needs to breathe underwater. The prefects' bathroom, with its murals of mermaids, was where Harry discovered the initial clue about the breathing-underwater task. As the youngest and least popular Triwizard champion, with the suspicious eyes of everyone upon him, facing a seemingly impossible task, Harry feels utterly powerless and alone. The dream accurately reflects these feelings in the image of his prized Firebolt being snatched away by a mermaid, a creature of the water who looks down on him and mocks his impotence.

Harry's class on Divination, taught by Professor Trelawney, comes across as the least reliable branch of magical knowledge, appealing to gullible people willing to see omens of death and doom in every cup of tea leaves. Harry doesn't take Professor Trelawney seriously, but one afternoon toward the end of the story (in a chapter titled "The Dream") he falls asleep in her class and finds himself "riding on the back of an eagle owl, soaring through the clear blue sky toward an old, ivy-covered house set high on a hillside." Inside the house Harry comes upon Voldemort, his snake Nagini, and his bumbling servant Wormtail. He watches as Voldemort tortures Wormtail and promises Nagini he will soon be feeding on Harry Potter. His scar burning his forehead, Harry awakens to the whole class staring at him and Professor Trelawney breathlessly asking to hear what he just dreamed about.

Harry brushes her off and runs to tell Professor Dumbledore, the headmaster of Hogwarts. This time Harry has no doubt that his dream contains meaningful information for the anti-Voldemort forces. To his relief, Dumbledore accepts his dream as real and significant, explaining that the failed killing curse of the Dark Lord seems to have created a psychic connection between them. Harry asks, "So you think . . . that dream . . . did it really happen?" "It is possible," said Dumbledore. "I would say—probable."

This opens a new and profoundly dangerous dimension of dream experience for Harry. Beyond the post-traumatic nightmares, beyond the prophetic visions and performance anxiety dreams, he now finds himself in direct contact with the inner thoughts of the most evil wizard in the world.

Harry's dream-link with Voldemort becomes a central factor in the plot of the fifth book, *Harry Potter and the Order of the Phoenix*. This novel, the longest in the series (870 pages), begins with a new reason for Harry to suffer post-traumatic nightmares. The Triwizard tournament ended disastrously with another attack by Voldemort, leading to the death of Cedric Diggory, a Hogwarts student. It happened in a graveyard, and no one but Harry witnessed it, barely escaping death himself. As this novel opens Harry is still suffering the emotional aftershocks:

> It was bad enough that he kept revisiting the graveyard in his nightmares, without dwelling on it in his waking moments too. . . . [H]e had nothing to look forward to but another restless, disturbed night, because even when he escaped nightmares about Cedric he had unsettling dreams about long dark corridors, all finishing in dead ends and locked doors, which he supposed had something to do with the trapped feeling he had when he was awake.

This corridor scenario reappears in Harry's dreams throughout the book. The simultaneous prickling of his scar indicates a connection to Voldemort, but for most of the story it's unclear to Harry and the readers where these recurrent dreams are leading.

Early in the story Harry arrives at the secret headquarters of the Order of the Phoenix, whose members are pledged to defeat Voldemort. On his first night there, after a warm reunion with his friends and teachers, Harry falls asleep to the sound of people walking on the stairs outside his room:

> In fact, many-legged creatures were cantering softly up and down outside the bedroom door, and Hagrid, the Care of Magical Creatures teacher, was saying, "Beauties, aren't they, eh Harry? We'll be studying weapons this term. . . ." And Harry saw that the creatures had cannons for heads and were wheeling to face him. . . . He ducked.

The silliness of this dream reflects Harry's relatively low anxiety level at the moment. For a brief interlude he feels safe and protected; he's able to relax enough to indulge in the whimsical freedom of dreaming. Of course, there's always something more going on—the cantering, weapon-bearing, many-legged creatures familiar to his friend Hagrid turn out to be anticipations of the book's final battle when a troop of arrow-shooting centaurs rescue Harry and save the day.

The night before he takes the train to school he has another odd dream in which old fears and new concerns push their way back into his sleeping mind: "Harry had a troubled night's sleep. His parents wove in and out of his dreams, never speaking; Mrs. Weasley sobbed over Kreacher's dead body watched by Ron and Hermione, who were wearing crowns, and yet again Harry found himself walking down a corridor ending in a locked door." Kreacher, another victim of Voldemort's, was a house elf loyal to Harry; Ron and Hermione have been named prefects of their house, an honor that leaves Harry unexpectedly envious. He feels no closer to his parents, no more capable of defeating Voldemort, and no closer to the secret behind the closed door. The dream reflects his preoccupations as the new school term begins.

In Professor Trelawney's class on Divination this year the students are introduced to the practice of dream interpretation. I am sorry to report it does not go well. The students are assigned a book by Inigo Imago titled *The Dream Oracle*, which appears to be a symbol dictionary instructing readers to interpret dreams by calculating the age of the dreamer, the date of the dream, and the number of letters in the subject. Professor Trelawney tells her students "dream interpretation is a most important means of divining the future," but she offers no further guidance before setting them in pairs to interpret each other's dreams using the book. Not surprisingly, Harry has no patience with this and he simply makes up a dream rather than share a real one.

If Mr. Dursley represents one kind of dream ignorance, Professor Trelawney represents another. Her foolishness teaches readers how *not* to interpret dreams: not in a pressured public situation, not using a symbol dictionary, not ignoring the dreamer's personal feelings, not focusing always on omens of doom. Just when Harry could benefit from some trustworthy practical knowledge about dreaming, his Divination class makes the whole subject seem like a waste of time.

Nevertheless, the dreams of the corridor and the locked door increase in frequency, and each time Harry becomes more greedily curious to know what lies on the other side of the door. One night, right after his first kiss with a girl named Cho Chang, he has a "normal" dream that takes a suddenly terrifying turn. It starts out with Cho and the question of whether or not to give her his Firebolt as a gift; then

> The dream changed. . . . His body felt smooth, powerful, flexible. He was gliding between shining metal bars, across dark, cold stone. . . . He was flat against the floor, sliding along on his belly. . . . It was dark, yet he could see objects around him shimmering in strange, vibrant colors. . . . He was turning his head. . . . At first glance, the corridor was empty . . . but no . . . a man was sitting on the floor ahead, his chin drooping onto his chest, his outline gleaming in the dark. . . . Harry put out his tongue. . . . He tasted the man's scent on the air.

In the dream Harry rears up and bites the man; then he suddenly wakes up in panic, covered in sweat, his head throbbing, sick to his stomach. He immediately tells his friends and teachers that Mr. Weasley, Ron's father, is in danger—that was the man he bit in the dream. They keep asking if he's sure it wasn't "just" a dream. Harry urgently tries to explain: "I was having a dream at first about something completely different, something stupid . . . and then this interrupted it. It was real, I didn't imagine it." Eventually he gets to Professor Dumbledore, who believes Harry is telling the truth. The Order of the Phoenix springs into action and they save Mr. Weasley, who barely escapes Nagini with his life.

This experience gives Harry the strongest evidence yet that he can trust his dreams. (He skips over the "stupid" part about Cho and his Firebolt.) Ironically, this is the very moment when he should be most cautious, because Voldemort has now realized that Harry can see into his mind. Soon after saving Mr. Weasley, Harry goes to sleep and "it was as though a film in his head had been waiting to start." He walks down the corridor toward a plain black door, feeling an overwhelming need to reach the other side. This dream comes back to him again and again, even though Professor Dumbledore has told Harry he must learn the magical art of Occlumency to guard his mind: "[P]ractice [Occlumency] particularly every night before sleeping so that you can close your mind to bad dreams—you will understand soon enough, but you must promise me—remember, close your mind—you will understand."

But the truth is, Harry is intrigued by the dreams and he wants more than anything to know where that door leads—"He was quite keen for the dreams to continue." This makes him an easy target for the Dark Lord. During his final exam in History of Magic, Harry falls asleep and slips into a dream where he sees Voldemort in the Ministry of Magic torturing Sirius. Harry awakens in a panic and persuades all his friends to rush to Sirius's rescue. It turns out to be an ambush—Voldemort has been using Harry's dreams to lure him to this very place to kill him. In the ensuing battle Sirius dies, and afterward Harry feels intensely guilty: "If he had not been stupid enough to fall for Voldemort's trick, if he had not been so convinced that what he had seen in his dream was real." To his woe, Harry learns that the prophetic power of dreaming brings with it a dangerous potential for deception and misinterpretation. He was all too willing to believe another dream was calling him to play the hero, a noble but uncritical impulse Voldemort used to seduce him into a fatal mistake.

Two more novels remain in the series, but the role of dreaming diminishes after its peak of significance in *The Order of the Phoenix*. In the sixth book, *Harry Potter and the Half-Blood Prince*, Harry begins dreaming of Ron's younger sister Ginny, signaling the love interest that will carry him to the end. He has a brief anxiety dream about Ron's displeasure at their relationship, and a broken series of images of Draco Malfoy, Professor Snape, and Professor Slughorn, another Slytherin teacher. At the end of the book, when he must prepare for the final battle against Voldemort, he dreams of the challenges ahead: "[H]is dreams were thick with cups, lockets, and mysterious objects that he could not quite reach, though Dumbledore helpfully offered Harry a rope ladder that turned to snakes the moment he began to climb." The outerworld challenges have come to the fore, and the narrative focuses less on Harry's inner world and more on the external task of finding these magical objects that will enable him to kill Voldemort.

The final book, *Harry Potter and the Deathly Hallows*, leads up to the inevitable duel-to-the-death between Harry and the Dark Lord. Along the way Harry has another clairvoyant dream about Voldemort's real-time activities. His friend Hermione warns him against trusting his dreams; "I didn't mean it to happen," Harry says. "It was a dream. Can YOU control what you dream about, Hermione?" Apparently lucid dreaming is not a wizarding skill.

Later, during a tense night in hiding, "Harry's dreams were confused and disturbing: Nagini wove in and out of them, first through a gigantic cracked ring, then through a wreath of Christmas roses." The cracked ring refers to a magical object that killed Dumbledore, and the wreath to Harry's sadness at missing the comforts of a Christmas family holiday. Voldemort, represented by his serpent, is directly responsible for these aching emotional holes in Harry's life.

Other than those brief mentions, dreams play little part in the climactic battle that consumes the rest of the seventh book. The prophetic visions of his dreaming mind can only carry him so far. After that, Harry must act in the waking world. This has been Professor Dumbledore's message all along. In the first book of the series, when Harry becomes excessively enchanted with images of his parents reflected in the Mirror of Erised, Dumbledore warns him, "It does not do to dwell on dreams and forget to live, remember that." At the end of the seventh book a ghostly vision of Dumbledore confesses his own guilt in pursuing magical power at all costs, telling Harry it was "a desperate man's dream!" His use of "dream" as a metaphor to describe vain, selfish desires is a reminder to Harry and his readers that no matter how exciting and compelling one's dreams may feel, there's real work to be done in the waking world. It's a paradoxical message to find in a work of fantasy fiction, but it's true to J. K. Rowling's portrayal of magic as a source of ancient wisdom and power that can be a source of good or evil, depending on one's choices and actions in life.

# Appendix 4

## ACTIVITIES TO STIMULATE WONDER IN CHILDHOOD

One of the distinct joys of parenthood is the opportunity to encourage a healthy and balanced relationship between our children's developing egos and the ancient archetypal wisdom flowing from the collective unconscious. Dreaming is one of the primary ways of maintaining and strengthening this balance, and we hope readers will now feel empowered to explore their own dreams and the dreams of their children. We want to close by mentioning some of the many other activities and experiences that can also promote children's capacity to find meaning, insight, and wonder in the world.

What follows is a collection of wonder-provoking activities that parents and children can enjoy together. While compiling this list we were reminded that the joy of childhood is delightfully wrapped up in a playful process of exploration and discovery. These activities cost little or nothing and can be tucked into a busy day or drawn out for a lazy weekend. Each one can be adapted for a particular age or for multiple ages if you have a group. The point is simply to enjoy these precious adventures of the imagination.

- Lie on your backs at the park and make animal shapes out of clouds.
- Build up a collection of clothing, wigs, and props to use for make-believe. Act out stories for fun.

- Make forts with sheets and blankets draped over chairs and couches. Take a nap there with your pillow, favorite blanket, toys, and a flashlight.
- Go to the local library, especially on story day. Look for books about subjects you've never read about before.
- Go to a lake, river, or pond, or to the ocean. Wiggle your toes in the water. Watch for little creatures and look at them carefully.
- Draw a map of your immediate neighborhood with familiar places marked. Then walk around the neighborhood following your map. Add places of interest like a big tree, a fire hydrant, or a cracked sidewalk.
- Draw the planets to scale and cut them out. Tack them up on your bedroom ceiling and imagine flying from one to the other in a spaceship. Learn the names of the planets.
- Start learning a different language, a few words at a time. Listen carefully to a certain bird and see if you can figure out a few words of its language. A crow is a good one for this.
- Visit a factory and see how something is put together or made. Then look at something in your house, like a toy or a piece of furniture, and try to imagine how it was made.
- Learn to swim, especially in the ocean if possible.
- Build a little fire (in a safe place!) and watch the ever-changing shapes of the flames. Are they dancing?
- Go to a place where you can roll down a grassy hill. Do it again and again. Can you roll up?
- Visit some elderly people regularly and ask them to tell you stories about what it was like when they were young.
- Go out after dark, lie on a blanket, and look up at the stars. Do you see the Dippers? Now listen carefully for night sounds.
- When an appropriate opportunity presents itself, talk a little about death. Answer simple questions with simple answers.

Be prepared not to know all the answers. Your heart will tell you what to say.

- Take a walk and imagine that a thousand years ago people and animals were walking on the same exact ground. Can the dirt below your feet possibly be that old? Even older?
- Watch a cat or a dog while it's sleeping. What's happening with their eyes, whiskers, paws, tails? What do you think they might be dreaming about?

# Appendix 5

## QUESTIONS FOR A
## STUDY GROUP OR BOOK CLUB
## ON CHILDREN'S DREAMS

Joining and participating in a small study group is a delightful way to learn more about the dynamics and meanings of dreams. People often have interesting dreams and wonder what they mean. When you take that dream to your dream group you have the opportunity to tell it out loud and have others explore the images and metaphors with you. Following Jung's amplification model you would analyze the dream structure first and then look at the various themes, metaphors, and archetypes. Everyone takes a turn expressing their ideas and feelings, prefacing their comments by saying, "If this was my dream, that would mean x to me." Only the dreamer can make the deeper associations and personal connections, but the group can be very helpful in teasing out the various possibilities.

With children, the value of participating in a dream group depends on their age. For younger children, their parents would likely hear the dream first and write it down. The youngster could then work with the dream by drawing a dream character or acting out the story. The parent could then take that dream to a study group and let the other members explore it together. As children grow they may want a dream group of their own. An interested teacher or parent could guide the group as the kids get used to telling and exploring each other's dreams.

Another possibility would be for readers to form a dream group to discuss each chapter of this book and present dreams they or their children have had in order to become familiar with Jung's amplification process. We believe that studying actual dreams in a group setting is the best way to make the information in our book come alive for you. We can talk about dreams, but only you can experience them, understand them, and put their insights into practice in your life.

The first and most important activity for a person who wants to study dreams is "dream catching." The key here is to get yourself set up *before* you go to bed. Put out a blank book or piece of paper and a pencil right next to the bed. When you wake up with the memory of a dream, write it down right away before you get up to do something else. Dreams have a way of drifting off into thin air. You literally have to catch them.

The same is true for children. Make sure they have a pad of paper and a pen or pencil at their bedside. If you like, you can help your children create a dream journal with an artistic cover and specially designed pages to fill in whenever they remember a dream. When you kiss your children good night say, "Sweet dreams!" First thing in the morning, go ahead and ask them if they can remember a dream. If not, that's fine, just go on with your regular morning routine. If yes, write it down as soon as you can. If you have had a dream and it feels appropriate, you can share it with your children and ask them what they think of it. This will allow the children to become familiar with hearing dreams (as most children in indigenous cultures through history have done). You can also ask them to pretend it was their dream and ask what they would have done or felt in those circumstances. Making a game out of it will capture their imaginations and spark their eagerness to tell their own dreams.

Now that you are collecting dreams, you are ready to gather your group for the first meeting. Each group will function differently depending on its purpose. Decisions will have to be made as to time, dates, place, and so on. An easy agenda would be: check-in, group discussion using the study guide topics for each chapter, and then one or two people sharing a dream for the group to discuss using Jung's model of amplification.

What follows are some group discussion topics for each chapter.

## INTRODUCTION

Go around the group, introducing yourself if necessary, and say a few words about why you are interested in learning about children's dreams.

Choose one or two dreams from chapter 3. Read them out loud and discuss as a group the qualities of wonder, connection, and future preparation revealed in them.

How important is the parent's initial response when a child reports a dream or nightmare?

## CHAPTER 1: INTERPRETING CHILDREN'S DREAMS

Go over figures 1, 2, and 3 to be sure everyone in the group understands the *psychological structures* represented by the drawings.

Review the vocabulary of Jung's approach: collective unconscious, culture, archetypes, ego, personal unconscious, the prospective function, the compensatory function.

We are focusing on children's "big dreams" in this book. Talk in the group about the difference between big dreams and little dreams. Give examples.

Have each person take a clean sheet of paper or a clean page in their dream journal and write down Jung's four-part method of analyzing a dream (Locale, Exposition, Peripeteia, and Lysis). Now have someone present a dream and the group will write down the structure of the dream according to Jung's outline, talking together as you go. Then continue the analysis by discussing archetypes and metaphors. You can look ahead to chapter 3 for examples of this process. Use your own dreams until you have collected some children's dreams.

## CHAPTER 2: BRAIN SCIENCE, DREAMS, AND THE IMAGINATION

Some very important discoveries have been made recently in the field of brain research. We mentioned six:

Brain structure
Social cognition
Sleep
Play
Emotions
Metaphor

Have each person take one or two sections and describe in a few sentences what the new findings are and how they help you understand child development.

Now have someone who has not shared before present a dream. Using Jung's process, first look at the structure of the dream and then notice any meanings arising from archetypal material.

## CHAPTER 3: DREAMS OF EARLY CHILDHOOD (AGES THREE TO FIVE)

Now you can read several dreams and their analyses using amplification. Go over these dreams one at a time so that you become very familiar with the process. Point out things that surprise you. Comment on ideas you would add or interpretive paths you would follow.

Ask two people to be ready to present fresh dreams. Now try the four-part analysis and amplification again. Does it seem easier?

## CHAPTER 4: DREAMS OF MIDDLE CHILDHOOD (AGES SIX TO NINE)

Somebody read the first two paragraphs of chapter 4 and spend some time discussing with the group the difference in dream content and dynamics between early childhood and middle childhood.

In Ann Marie's dream we consider the samurai warriors to be archetypal. Why do we think that?

Discuss the value of self-reflection for children six to nine years old.

Look at the bicycle symbols in Hector's and Ben's dreams. How do they compare?

What is the challenge for Inge in the "Girl of the Rainbow" dream?

Analyze a dream from the group. Hopefully you are using children's dreams now or big dreams remembered by members of the group.

## CHAPTER 5: DREAMS OF LATE CHILDHOOD AND EARLY ADOLESCENCE (NINE AND OLDER)

Do you remember any puberty dreams you had? Describe one to your group. Was the dream helpful, embarrassing, super strange? Did you tell anyone about it when you first dreamed it?

Did you have a recurring dream growing up? Tell the group about the dream and how it changed and developed as you and your life changed.

How would you talk with the girl who had the dream of rats in her sister's dress? Was it like a little kid's nightmare?

Have you ever had an experience of breathtaking awe and existential fear at seeing something so big you realize that you are just a tiny inconsequential speck in the great scheme of things? In the last cluster of dreams in our book we focus on the titanic dreams some children experience. Suddenly they are faced with paradoxes and truths all children eventually must embrace. They are growing up, and finally getting big. At the same time, they begin to realize how fragile and short life is. Discuss in the group how these cosmic dreams express such existential insights. What would you say to a young person who has had a titanic dream?

## CHAPTER 6: NURTURING THE IMAGINATION IN CHILDHOOD AND BEYOND

Review your progress in learning how to record dreams and keep them together in a journal. Continue to add notes about the analysis of that dream and perhaps add to it again over time.

Have you successfully written down some of your children's dreams? You might want to continue working with the themes of these dreams in their waking life.

Where do you find wonder and creativity in your life? You will do a better job of nurturing your children's imaginations if you take care of your own yearnings for wonder, play, and discovery. Children learn so much more from what we do than from what we say.

If you have a baby, you will have to wait for the little one to get old enough to describe a dream. On that exciting day you will be ready with your "Child's Dream Journal" to begin collecting what Jung called "the richest jewels in the treasure house of the soul."

# REFERENCES AND SUGGESTED READINGS

## INTRODUCTION

Many of the ideas and practices in this book are discussed in our previous coauthored book, *Dreaming Beyond Death: A Guide to Pre-Death Dreams and Visions* (Boston: Beacon Press, 2008). Kelly's work *The Wondering Brain: Thinking about Religion With and Beyond Cognitive Neuroscience* (New York: Routledge, 2005) goes into more detail about several topics we mention in this book: wonder, dreams, neuroscience, pragmatism, and artistic creativity, to name a few.

Other good books on children's dreams include *Dreamguider: Open the Door to Your Child's Dreams* by Denyse Beaudet (Newburyport, MA: Hampton Roads, 2008); *Your Child's Dreams* by Patricia Garfield (New York: Ballantine Books, 1984); and *Dreamcatching: Every Parent's Guide to Exploring and Understanding Children's Dreams and Nightmares* by Alan Siegel and Kelly Bulkeley (New York: Three Rivers Press, 1998).

## CHAPTER 1: INTERPRETING CHILDREN'S DREAMS

Jung's childhood dream is presented in his autobiography, *Memories, Dreams, Reflections* (New York: Vintage, 1965) (translated by Richard and Clara Winston), pp. 11–12, 15. Good biographies of Jung include *Jung and the Story of Our Time* (New York: Vintage Books,

1976) by Laurens Van Der Post, and *Jung: A Biography* (Back Bay Books, 2004) by Deirdre Bair. For advanced studies in Jungian psychology, see *Jung in the 21st Century,* vol. 1: *Evolution and Archetype,* and vol. 2: *Synchronicity and Science* (New York: Routledge, 2010), by John R. Haule, and *Teaching Jung* (New York: Oxford University Press, 2011), edited by Kelly Bulkeley and Clodagh Weldon.

If you really want to understand Jung's ideas about dreams, you should read Sigmund Freud's *The Interpretation of Dreams,* which has been published in many translations (we prefer the James Strachey version).

The Jung seminars are published in *Children's Dreams: Notes from the Seminar Given in 1936–1940* (Princeton: Princeton University Press, 2008) (translated by Ernst Falzeder and Tony Woolfson). The quotes come from pp. 7, 19, 26, 28, 31, 70, 238. The quote about dreams being a part of nature comes from *Memories, Dreams, Reflections,* pp. 161–162.

CHAPTER 2: BRAIN SCIENCE,
DREAMS, AND THE IMAGINATION

For information on brain structure, see *The Brain: A Neuroscience Primer* (Worth Publishers, 2000) by Richard H. Thompson. The quote comes from p. 3. For more on current studies of the unconscious, see *The New Unconscious* (New York: Oxford University Press, 2006), edited by Ran R. Hassin, James S. Uleman, and John A. Bargh; the quote comes from pp. 37–38. Another good book on the brain, emotion, and social cognition is *The Feeling of What Happens: Body and Emotion in the Making of Consciousness* (San Diego: Harcourt, 1999), with the quote from p. 228.

General information about sleep can be found at the website of the National Sleep Foundation (www.sleepfoundation.org). For information about dreaming, see the website of the International Association for the Study of Dreams (www.asdreams.org).

Another good source on dream research is G. William Domhoff's *The Scientific Study of Dreams: Neural Networks, Cognitive Development, and Content Analysis* (Washington, DC: American Psychological Association Press, 2003). Revonsuo's threat-simulation theory of dreaming can be found in *Sleep and Dreaming: Scientific Advances and Reconsiderations* (New York: Cambridge University Press, 2003), edited by Edward F. Pace-Schott, Mark Solms, Mark Blagrove, and Stevan Harnad. On metaphor, our main source is *Metaphors We Live By* (Chicago: University of Chicago Press, 1984), with a quote from p. 5. The Lakoff quote on dreams comes from an article he wrote titled "How Metaphor Structures Dreams," reprinted in a book Kelly edited, *Dreams: A Reader on the Religious, Cultural, and Psychological Dimensions of Dreaming* (New York: Palgrave, 1999), p. 274.

Research on children's dreams comes from David Foulkes's *Children's Dreaming and the Development of Consciousness* (Cambridge, MA: Harvard University Press, 1999); G. William Domhoff's *Finding Meaning in Dreams: A Quantitative Approach* (New York: Plenum Press, 1996); Kate Adams in *The Spiritual Dimension of Childhood* (London: Jessica Kingsley, 2008) (coauthored with B. Hyde and R. Woolley); and Kelly's article "Earliest Remembered Dreams," in the journal *Dreaming* (2005, vol. 15, no. 3, pp. 205–222) (coauthored with Bitsy Broughton, Anita Sanchez, and Joanne Stiller). The quote comes from p. 220. The Adams quote comes from a book she, Kelly, and Patricia M. Davis coedited, *Dreaming in Islam and Christianity: Culture, Conflict, Creativity* (New Brunswick, NJ: Rutgers University Press, 2009), p. 223.

## CHAPTER 3: DREAMS OF EARLY CHILDHOOD

Sam's dream life is discussed in more detail in Kelly's book *American Dreamers: What Dreams Tells Us about the Political Psychology of Conservatives, Liberals, and Everyone Else* (Boston: Beacon Press,

2008; in which he is referred to as Will). The Brian Aldiss dream report comes from *The Tiger Garden: A Book of Writers' Dreams* (London: Serpent's Tail, 1996), pp. 4–5. The dream from Jung's seminar is described on pp. 135–150.

## CHAPTER 4: DREAMS OF MIDDLE CHILDHOOD

Richard's dream life is discussed in more detail in *American Dreamers*. The dream from Jung's seminar is described on pp. 124–132. The quote comes from p. 128. Ben's bicycle dreams were first presented in Kelly's book with Alan Siegel, *Dreamcatching*.

## CHAPTER 5: DREAMS OF LATE CHILDHOOD AND EARLY ADOLESCENCE

The dream practices of the Sambia of New Guinea, the Ojibwa of North America, and other indigenous cultures can be found in Kelly's work *Dreaming in the World's Religions: A Comparative History* (New York: New York University Press, 2008). The dream from Jung's seminar is described on pp. 32–41. Paul's dream life is discussed in more detail in *American Dreamers*. The dreams of Lawrence Watt-Evans and John Gordon come from *The Tiger Garden,* pp. 235–236 and 91–92. The dreams of Trudy and Ronnie come from the "Earliest Remembered Dreams" article.

## CHAPTER 6: NURTURING THE IMAGINATION IN CHILDHOOD AND BEYOND

For more on dream-sharing, see *Dream Work* (Mahwah: Paulist Press, 1983); *Where People Fly and Water Runs Uphill* (New York: Warner Books, 1993) by Jeremy Taylor; and *Working with Dreams* (New York: HarperCollins, 1989) by Montague Ullman and Nan

Zimmerman. More ideas for teachers can be found in a book coauthored by Kelly, Phil King, and Bernard Welt, *Dreaming in the Classroom: Practices, Methods, and Resources in Dream Education* (Albany: State University of New York Press, 2011). Clara Hill's work can be found in *Working with Dreams in Psychotherapy* (New York: Guilford Press, 1996); and Clara Hill, ed., *Dream Work in Therapy: Facilitating Exploration, Insight, and Action* (Washington, DC: American Psychological Association, 2003).

# INDEX

# ABOUT THE AUTHORS

**Kelly Bulkeley** is visiting scholar at the Graduate Theological Union, senior editor of the journal *Dreaming*, and former president of the International Association for the Study of Dreams. He received a Ph.D. in religion and psychological studies from the University of Chicago Divinity School. He has written and edited several books on dream research. His most recent works are *Dreaming in the World's Religions: A Comparative History, American Dreamers: What Dreams Tell Us about the Political Psychology of Conservatives, Liberals, and Everyone Else*, and *Dreaming in Christianity and Islam: Culture, Conflict, and Creativity* (coedited with Kate Adams and Patricia M. Davis). In 2010 he created the Sleep and Dream Database, a digital archive and search engine designed to advance the empirical study of dreams. Kelly lives in Portland, Oregon, with his wife and three children. His website and blog is at http://kellybulkeley.com.

**Patricia M. Bulkley** is a former interfaith spiritual services director at Hospice of Marin and a teacher in the pastoral counseling program of San Francisco Theological Seminary. She earned a doctor of ministry degree from Princeton Theological Seminary, writing her dissertation on dreams of the dying and their psychological and spiritual impact on the dreamer's actual death. For the past thirty-five years, she has been counseling and teaching at SFTS and other Bay Area institutions on topics of interfaith spirituality, family psychology, and community caregiving. For the past several years she has been studying Jung's psychology as a resource in spiritual counseling throughout the lifespan, from early childhood into old age. Patricia lives in Sonoma, California, with her husband and a variety of pets and farm animals.

Together, Kelly and Patricia are the authors of the book *Dreaming Beyond Death: A Guide to Pre-Death Dreams and Visions.*

CPSIA information can be obtained at www.ICGtesting.com
Printed in the USA
BVOW031723290712

296439BV00001B/5/P